MODERN
EUROPEAN PAINTING

MODERN
EUROPEAN PAINTING

by
ALFREDO COLOMBO

Translated by
IDA B. PULAY

CASTLE BOOKS · NEW YORK 10, N.Y.

Published by

CASTLE BOOKS

NEW YORK 10, N. Y.

by arrangement with

Istituto Geografico De Agostini S.p.A. • Novara, Italy

English language text © Books for Pleasure Ltd 1961

PRINTED IN ITALY

VINCENT VAN GOGH: Crows over a Cornfield (detail)
V. W. van Gogh Collection, Amsterdam

PREFACE

The period in European painting considered in this volume is of the greatest interest and importance for us today. It has seen the decay of one academic tradition and the growth of another. At the beginning of the nineteenth century the Renaissance basis of art was unchallenged and seemingly unchallengeable, but before the century closed it was clearly destined to be superseded. This aesthetic development is a constant and continuing natural process and is not remarkable in itself. As is usual, it has been accompanied by the incomprehension and antagonism of those born into and formed by the earlier aesthetic. This too is a normal condition; one may imagine the mediaeval Italian being appalled by Renaissance humanism on its appearance and looking longingly back to the certainty and comfort of the old religion. Each succeeding change has to face the antagonism of its predecessor, and we should not be surprised that 'modern art' is reviled and rejected. Nor is it surprising if the public is bewildered and suspects that an intellectual confidence trick is being played on it; the creative activity is an isolated thing in which the public cannot participate and it will always wear an air of mystery.

The situation is somewhat complicated today by the radical and seemingly historically unrelated changes that have occurred. Not only has the Renaissance aesthetic been rejected but there seems to be no connection between it and the 'modern' aesthetic. Most people, one supposes, would still acknowledge that there must be a connection but they are unable to discern it. This strengthens the suspicion of deceit and insincerity. It is sometimes forgotten that the forms of art do not emerge casually from a temporary fashion or condition but lie deep in society and its complex relationship to the physical world. It may thus be valuable to the background of this book to comment on the nature of this 'modern' aesthetic and indicate its relationship to the great pervading aesthetic of the Renaissance.

The Renaissance aesthetic was concerned with the nature of man's competence in the face of an intricate Nature, secret and wonderful but essentially comprehensible. It sought to place man at the physical, mental and spiritual centre of Nature; it made man the yardstick of Nature. In art this reflected itself in a desire to show man's command over Nature, to indicate his potential for perfection. Thus the Renaissance artist sought perfection of representation, suggesting the notion, embedded in man's primitive nature, that this command of representation would give him power over the object represented—in this case the whole physical world. This overriding competence was what the Renaissance artist was always claiming for himself as excellence. Thus Vasari, the Renaissance art historian, again and again gauges greatness.

Unfortunately for our simple acceptance of this as the basis of the Renaissance aesthetic, there is another important factor in its formation. Renaissance man was also bound up with his rediscovery of the Classical societies of Greece and Rome and his identification with their ideas and concepts; he began to equate his intellectual prowess and cultural adulthood with his knowledge of Classical philosophy, drama, poetry and art. The result was an attempt, variously successful, to overlay his competence in the representation of the visible world with an interpretation of subject matter in the light of Classical studies, secular, mythological, religious—a sort of intellectual exhibitionism. Thus, to cut a long process short, appearance became subject to form, form bred virtuosity, virtuosity in its turn bred arrogance, arrogance bred ignorance, and ignorance conservatism.

The inadequacy of this debased aesthetic began to be apparent to some inquisitive and creative spirits in France during the middle years of the nineteenth century and from their disquiet at the perverted intellectualism of the masters of the academies, the first modern movement, Impressionism, emerged. Since the Impressionists were somewhat pallid revolutionaries, their notions were in turn attacked by their successors until the end of the century.

On this ground the twentieth century has laid a new aesthetic, removing man from the optimistic centre of affairs, competent and Olympian, and reducing him to one creature among many, struggling with the simplest relationships, technologically advanced but insensitive and confined in his mental life and primitive in the extreme in his social life. As knowledge has increased, wisdom has lagged; knowledge has nevertheless lent humility to realize limitations—the void gets larger, man is less sure, truth is relative, the eternal verities become mumbo-jumbo. We do not know where or who we are, the only certain thing is uncertainty.

In art this has resulted in the removal of all the props that buttressed its position. The esteem which likeness in representation has lent for centuries—and the assurance that recognition and nostalgia give—has withered to bragga-docio. Artists have begun the search for the simple relationships that, no longer certain of anything, they need to build upon. They have destroyed the existing order with callous indifference and guyed the pretensions of the Re-naissance with the defiance of children; the moustache on the Mona Lisa was no doodle, it was Marcel Duchamp's deliberate shattering of the halo. The new aesthetic is based on the hope of the existence of underlying order and a statement of faith that it will be found. It is an attack on man's pretensions. It is not nihilistic; it is courageous and hopeful.

One last word: whilst the divorce between the people and the artist is in some measure unavoidable, it is none-theless unfortunate and is not of the artist's seeking. He wishes closer contact, since only thus can he have his effect. As Paul Klee has said, 'We still lack the ultimate power: for the people are not with us. But we seek a people... more we cannot do.'

Frederick Dawe

CLAUDE MONET: The Seine at Rouen (water-colour)

I

In Victor Hugo's writings we find a page, or rather a whole chapter, in which he proclaims with romantic exuberance that the nineteenth century has had no ancestors. Its mother, he maintains, was an idea—the French Revolution.

A standpoint as untenable by historic standards as this birth certificate (if you want to call it that) is a wilfully forged document and is not to be taken seriously. Victor Hugo wrote these lines in 1865, when in in exile at Hautville House. How could he have been driven to such an emphatic statement? This question can only be answered if one knows what the cultural climate of Europe was like at that time. It would seem to have been charged with electricity. The whole Continent had in the preceding decades been strongly influenced by various trends. There was first the Romantic movement, which was started in Germany by the Schlegels (1798), and by Novalis and Schliermacher; after that—also stemming from Germany—the powerful impact made by the works of Schiller, Goethe, Wieland and Tieck; and finally Coleridge's and Wordsworth's poetry, which had revolutionised English literature. The real initiator of this revolution was, one might say, Macpherson (1738—1796), with his allegedly old Celtic *Songs of Ossian*.

Romanticism in France, on the other hand, was sparked off by Mme de Staël's *De l'Allemagne*, the 'Manifesto of the French Romantic Movement', as it was called. As publication of it had been forbidden in its country of origin, it was published in London in 1813. In the Northern and Central European countries Romanticism began as a nationalistic movement, a quasi return to the origin of things. In the Latin countries it was opposed to traditional approaches and headed towards unknown, only intuitively grasped, aims—all in

EDOUARD MANET: Mademoiselle Victorine as a Spanish Dancer (pencil drawing)

favour of new trends. In literature, every accepted idea which had had its origin in the pattern of antiquity was fought against, and every trend which did not stem directly from life or history and did not concern itself with deeper moral issues was rejected. In short, the spirit of the time wished to express itself in a realistic way. The quintessence of Romanticism lies in an inner, purely inspirational, form which is the link between poetry and life. It would, therefore, appear to be a violent reaction against those intellectual movements which originated in Humanism and the Renaissance and reached their peak with the Enlightenment, whose aim it was to 'enlighten' by reason. Romanticism represents the mystical versus the real. It puts the objective truth of science in juxtaposition with an intrinsic hidden truth, and thus attempts to elevate the universe to a higher ethical plane. Determinism was made to see eye to eye with freedom which was to pave the way to permanent values.

As romantic aestheticism started on these ethical principles, it did as a matter of course reflect a new sense of life, 'in which the secret forces of nature which also direct the human being were of the highest value.' Thus rigid, abstract rules became gradually looser; this helped the imagination to gain a creative freedom which dispensed with all regulations.

'The one and only origin of the diverse artistic, philosophical and social movements of the nineteenth century', said Victor Hugo, 'is the French Revolution.' This statement, he thought, would exonerate his works from the reproach of being dated 'of 1793'. 'This new expression "the art of 1793" which, about 1830, in the time of Louis Philippe, was endlessly repeated, was meant to be a slight on the art of the day. It was not, however, by any means as insulting as intended. It was definitely unfair to disparage the whole movement by this new expression as far as the arts were concerned; and it was equally unfair to apply it to the political evolutions, as both these phenomena fundamentally embrace a much wider span than the year 1793. The term "literature of 1793" seems in some ways pertinent: it shows in spite of its vagueness and its insulting character where the sweeping movements of our time come from. The Revolution, this gigantic change in the life of mankind, lasted several years. Every one of these years marks an epoch, shows a different aspect, reveals a new phase of the event. If good news is sometimes announced by the roar of a cannon, 1793 is such a cannon. Be prepared! The first time God Himself spoke the words *fiat lux*. The second time He had them spoken. By whom? By the year 1793. Therefore we of the nineteenth century should feel honoured by the accusation, "You are of 1793." But this is not the end. We are just as much of '89 as of of '93. We are in fact the whole Revolution, and therefore the source of the art of the nineteenth century.' Although Victor Hugo avoids the word Romantic, it was a Romantic art. 'It is a battle-cry which expresses a number of ideas simultaneously and clearly: an advantage, it would appear. On the other hand it seems to me that by this very warlike quality the movement could be reduced to a mere war episode. Yet it is the intellectual, cultural and spiritual matters which are at stake here...'

And these spiritual matters were to have a vibrating influence on the literature and arts of half the European continent for some considerable time to come. To the artist this movement meant first of all liberation from academic rigidity, though later on it would create a new academic attitude all its own. It took on its specific hue in every country concerned, but was everywhere marked by the predominance of sentiment over reason and by a new value given to the human being both as an individual and as a member of a social group. There was more concern than ever before with human feelings and passions; sometimes this was expressed with pathos, but mostly in a lyrical, rather than a dramatic, way.

A new attitude towards pain, distress and rebellion made Romanticism not only a human but also a political movement. It awakened and liberated the spiritual forces which put themselves in the service of such needs as freedom, independence, law and justice, education of the masses and human solidarity.

Even where these needs were not a part of the public conscience and where the subject of art was not yet liberated from tradition, painters began to experiment with new techniques of light and colour and to explore new aesthetic approaches in order to get away from the stereotyped. With this they captivated the eye, the feeling and the mind of a public that up to then had been accustomed to attach more importance to line than colour. Many painters took to painting in the open air. Every brush-stroke became a canticle in praise of Nature, with whom they entered into a close and intimate, yet not irreverent, relationship. The personality of the artist became more and more evident in his paintings.

It was to take, of course, centuries before this evolution (which, according to Victor Hugo, could also be called a revolution) was completed. Even a century, and the art in which it expresses itself and by which it, in turn, is expressed, takes time to grow up. At the beginning of the nineteenth century, the years from 1789 to 1793 had not yet made their mark on art. This may have been because a retrograde phase had set in after Goya. Goya, a master of the Spanish Baroque, was a forerunner of Romanticism. His rather advanced style, however, was soon to be eclipsed by the Empire style: a Neoclassical movement which gave architecture, sculpture and music a respite before the sweep of real Romanticism.

This Neoclassicism had borrowed some of its elements from a former, long vanished and now revived, Empire style, whose aim had been the glorification of the Napoleonic era. Its effect, however, had reached far beyond that aim. Along with it had come an academic mannerism, which was not quite as cold and devoid of feeling as it had been accused of being. In spite of formalism, works of true form and colour, such as Canova's, Piermarini's and David's, were created. Such paintings as *Napoleon Crossing the Alps* and the *Coronation* by David, whose purpose it was to glorify Napoleon, had predecessors. As early as the time of Louis XVI there had been signs of a Neoclassicism, stimulated by the archaeological excavations at Pompeii and Herculaneum. The first, as yet undefined, symptoms of it can be found in some of Raphael Mengs' Roman paintings. Inner disruption of the art of the day paved the way for the new classicism, and though the French revolutionaries had Louis XVI executed, they yet willingly adopted a style that had pleased the tyrant. The king had liked the geometrical austerity of classical ornaments because he thought them majestic; the artists of the Revolution adopted them because the austerity of style to them seemed to reflect the sternness of Republican ideas.

So the revolutionaries wholeheartedly accepted David's *Oath of the Horatii* which had been painted in 1784, in Louis XVI's reign. David, that master of composition and portraiture, towered above most other painters of the Empire, such as Gros and Prud'hon. Yet Gros created real masterpieces, such as *Napoleon at the Battle of Eylau* and the *Pest House of Jaffa*. Prud'hon was a good colourist and a master of chiaroscuro, and his portrait of the *Empress Josephine* proves him a serious painter.

In the paintings of Gros (1771—1835) we feel the first stirrings of Impressionism. We must, however, not forget that Impressionism proper, as an artistic movement, began only forty years later, that it was intrinsically different from traditional European painting, that its influence went far beyond the French frontiers and that it led to a complete change, not only in painting, but also in sculpture, literature and criticism. It is generally acknowledged that Impressionism originated in this way: about 1870, several artists—among them Monet, Renoir and Pissarro—used to paint by the banks of the Seine and the Oise. They were realistic painters; they paid attention to the effect of light on water. They noticed that colours were separated in the transparent water, and that shadows cast by objects contain complementary colours. It was by spontaneous experience of real life and not by theoretical reasoning that they gave light to their palette and separated the tones on their canvases. At first they only painted water in the new way, with hills, trees, houses and the sky still in the old tradition. This gave their paintings an uneven effect. To counteract this, they tried to treat everything, including the human face, in the same way as they had treated water. Of all the elements which together constitute Nature they chose light alone to represent her. 'With them, light became the intrinsic principle of style: and with this Impressionism was born,' said Venturi. He added: 'Light is the element in which reality manifests itself, but what the Impressionists painted was not reality but its image. On this image they concentrated with more determination than any other painters before them. To understand it is, however, a matter of sensibility in which neither the conscious mind nor the will-power seems to have a part. Thus the Impressionists remained faithful to their sensibilities towards Nature and to their impressions of Nature, and found a method which did more justice to the fresh impression than any previous method of painting. This they achieved by an acute artistic awareness, and the knowledge of the absolute value of the image. They knew how to assess the true significance of their impressions and kept clear of tradition and abstract principles of form.' To this must be added one more rather important fact. Impressionism in its reaction to the objectivity of realism puts the personality of the artist in the foreground.

It has been said that Impressionism was a reaction against Romanticism, an opinion to which we do not wholly subscribe. The Impressionists, as we know, preferred to paint a cottage rather than a palace; simple girls rather than great ladies; workmen rather than aristocrats. This they did mostly out of a natural sympathy with the familiar elements of their own daily lives, which were the lives of poor country folk. The Romantics of course also painted peasants, simple girls and workmen, so one may say that Romanticism half opens a door to Impressionism. As Hartlaub says, '... many simultaneous movements in the history of the art of the nineteenth century eventually converge.'

In the years preceding the beginning and consolidation of a newly conscious 'programmatic art' as expressed in Impressionism, the critics had called some painters precursors of the movement. On closer inspection, however, one can see that even long before them Goya, as mentioned above, had shown a new, exciting, visual feeling for Nature: a certain way of representing her, a new vivacity in the movement of figures; a brighter scale of colours, new psychological details and a freer brush-stroke. One could go back to the very beginnings of art and find similar symptoms almost everywhere. Be it Caravaggio, or before him Guardi and Magnasco with their luminous canvases; be it the Early Christian paintings in the catacombs; or Roman art or even Hellenistic art and prehistoric murals—signs of the same feeling appear in all of them. Even if we went back into art history in that way, we would still not discover the true beginnings of Impressionism.

We have, however, only to go back a few years in time and a few miles in distance across the Channel. There we find Constable (1776—1837), assured and unassuming, yet with the most passionate eye for chiaroscuro and open spaces, a master of landscape painting. This calls to mind another school of English painting which had at last broken away from the influence of foreign masters (Holbein, Eworth, the Gheeraerts, Rubens, van Dyck, Lely, Watteau, Guardi and the Venetian and Bolognese Schools, as well as Correggio and Rembrandt). It is the period after Hogarth, Gainsborough and Reynolds. Gainsborough's technique was more brilliant and subtle than Reynolds', yet he had to assert himself against him. Gainsborough felt that England should have her own style of painting and he had the authority to introduce it, to maintain it and to pass it on. His works made landscape painting fashionable in his time. Wilson kept up the style, and the Norwich School, and John Crome in particular, went as far as banning everything that showed traces of Italian influence. Constable, without any knowledge of optics, was the first to render light with broken brush-strokes and broken patches of colour, thus giving his landscapes a sparkling life all their own; with this he became the real creator of Impressionism.

Much later, cultural exchange among artists of different countries became more universal. It was then that the English discovered Corot and Millet, and later Manet and Cézanne (who was to make the greatest impact of them all) and hailed them as pioneers of a new movement. They seemed to have forgotten that it was, in fact, they themselves who had created the movement and had been fifty years ahead of these Continental artists. Much later, Duncan Grant saw all this in true perspective; he became one of the pioneers of Post-Impressionism. But let us go back, for the time being, to France.

II

In 1824, at an exhibition of English paintings at the Paris Salon, the French became aware of Constable's technique and innovations. The subtly modulated atmosphere of the *Salisbury Cathedral* had a lyrical appeal all its own; here space and depth were suggested less by drawing than by choice of colour. The dimensions of reality were honoured, while its world had expanded and become lighter, more transparent. The French artists were willing disciples. The Barbizon School was formed, and settled in the woods near Paris—the same woods in which the earlier School of Fontainebleau had worked, standing up valiantly against the influence of Rosso and Primaticcio. The fight against academic formalism and studio painting had begun. After a time, Théodore Rousseau, Diaz, Harpignies, Daubigny, Troyon and Dupré took their easels to the river-banks, glades and mountain-sides. There they painted Nature as they saw her, but without as yet revealing their own temperament. The new means of expression were freedom from detail, a different brush-work and avoidance of depth. Rousseau and Dupré were the heads of this school, until Millet—a realistic painter at first—joined them and once more introduced the human figure. From then onwards man is given pride of place: masters like Daumier, Courbet and Sisley began to show a new social outlook.

At this point it seems appropriate to introduce Corot, who belongs to the same generation yet stands apart. He began as an academician, but in his long working life he was to pass through many different stages. The Impressionists can hardly claim him as one of them, let alone as one of the pioneers of the movement, and yet in his canvases, which are still peopled by the traditional mythological figures—nymphs and satyrs—a primary feeling for Nature can be felt, a new sense of harmony. Even though Corot was to remain on the outskirts of Impressionism, there is a foreshadowing of it in these paintings which assures him a place in the history of the movement. As he was one of the first artists to grope tentatively for the new, we should try to understand his importance and development.

J. B. C. Corot (1796—1875) was the son of a barber in the Rue du Bac near the Pont Royal where his mother kept a millinery shop. He was to be apprenticed to a tailor. His mother was a warm-hearted, understanding woman, his father a mild and optimistic man, and, eventually, they let him have painting lessons. He was first advised by an unknown artist, Michallon, then by Victor Bertin. Neither of them could teach him much. He was a born artist and as such went his own original way. At the age of twenty he first became acquainted with Constable's paintings. Upon that he joined the Barbizon School and began to roam the Paris suburbs and the country round. He also worked in Rouen and Ville d'Avray where the family owned a little house. In 1825 he went to Italy for two years.

Corot's first works, nearly all small landscapes, are reproduced in Moreau-Nélaton's *Corot, Raconté par Lui-même*, and in Robaut's understanding biography. Other well-known critics, such as Baudelaire, took an interest in him, and in the end all art critics and art historians began to concern themselves with his work. Some say that his origins were Neoclassical; others categorically claim him for Romanticism; others again see him as a realistic painter and maintain that he has a place in the development of Impressionist technique and aesthetics.

In the same generalising way in which were later to call Corot the link between Poussin and Cézanne, the critics now talked about two different Corots—a ' French ' one and an ' Italian ' one.

Corot exhibited his paintings at the Salon of 1827. Through contact with the Italian countryside and its limpid atmosphere he had both technically and sentimentally developed a style of his own. It was a pure classical style to which, however, the subtlety of new light effects gave a new freshness. These pictures were of a simple grandeur. After his return to Paris, Corot seldom worked in his studio in the Rue Voltaire. He travelled to Ville d'Avray, to Normandy, to Picardy and Burgundy. Between 1834 and 1843 he frequently went to Italy. Later, when old and famous, he visited Belgium, Holland and Switzerland. The output of this long, much-travelled life was about two thousand paintings and many drawings and etchings. Some say that Corot's ' French ' canvases were stylistically freer than his ' Italian ' ones. This, however, is not so. The countryside is different; so is the light; and the hazy landscape may have inspired pictures which were a prelude to Cézanne and to the mists of Monet—no more than a prelude, however.

Corot was no theoretician; had he been one he would have been better equipped to explain the split in his own nature. The real question seems to be this: should a picture be complete and finished to the last detail as classical rules decree, or should the painter, according to realistic tenets, be allowed to disregard detail, and by light and shadow only catch the essence of his subject? Corot was a meticulous technician. ' When I prepare a sketch,' he says, ' I begin by putting the lighter tones on to the white canvas—in their right order—there are about twenty different nuances between the lighter and darker tones. This is the way to start sketches or paintings properly...' He adds, however, ' ...that this order should never impair the freedom of line or colour. One should always keep in mind the whole of the picture and never lose the freshness of the first impression.'

At the beginning of his career Corot met with bitter disappointment. The public did not understand paintings which were later to be found in museums throughout the world. Though men like Delacroix, Burger-Thoré and Edouard About had enough foresight to anticipate the future master, they as yet had no power to influence public taste.

Honoré Daumier: The Laundress (1845, Louvre, Paris)

JEAN BAPTISTE CAMILLE COROT: Self-portrait (Uffizi, Florence)

GUSTAVE COURBET: Young Girl (Louvre, Paris)

Jean Baptiste Camille Corot: Agostina (1866, National Gallery of Art, Washington)

JEAN LOUIS FORAIN: Before the Judge (engraving)

The public, it is true, was not as hostile towards Corot as they were later to be towards Manet, Courbet and other pioneers who by then had taken to painting other subjects than landscapes in the new manner. This went so far that when Courbet, at the Salon of 1855, showed a painting of a peasant girl, the Empress Eugénie was so annoyed by his choice of subject that she poked at the picture with her umbrella. Courbet's technique, also far removed from the academic, brought him into conflict with public taste. This was the conflict, as Cogniet puts it, *'entre l'Institut figé dans son académisme et l'art vivant; conflit qui durera à peu près un siècle et l'on ne peut affirmer qu'il soit aujourd'hui terminé.'*

So Corot did what Constable did: he painted the same canvas twice. Once to the requirements of the Academy, the second time according to his own taste. (See *Da Giotto a Chagall* by Venturi.) There was no alternative to the above, other than to conform to the laws of the Academy and to irresolute public taste— which would have meant degradation and self-destruction as an artist—or be deprived of the rewards of one's work and excluded from the art market.

On this subject Venturi says: ' The original was a work of art, complete in itself if it gave the impression of light and shadow—regardless of the precise rendering of reality—i.e. complete from the artist's individual point of view, but incomplete in its representation of reality. The duplicate was painted in a naturalistic way. Colours, which in the original carried the effects of light, served in the duplicate only to fill in existing forms. A yellow field, luminous in the original, becomes flat in the duplicate. In the original, the silvery reflections of clouds on the water are in natural harmony with the brown refractions from the half-shadowy soil; in the duplicate the colour of the water becomes a monotonous greyish-green, which doesn't really give the shimmering effect of water...'

In the original every brush-stroke proclaimed that the artist was in sympathy with Nature. The duplicate was a mere reproduction of material reality. Both the Academy and the public were happy with these duplicates. They did not know that the artists had hidden away in their studios the magnificent originals which the public would not have understood, nor the members of the jury accepted. Later these original versions came into their own. The original of Corot's *Bridge of Narni* hangs in the Louvre; Constable's *Haywain*, in the National Gallery. The same applies to other originals.

We could conclude this chapter on Corot with a few anecdotes about his personal life which might throw some light on the way of living of painters at that time. It seems more important, however, to discuss once more the two so-called 'epochs' of his working life—the classical and the modern pre-Impressionist—as he did equally great and convincing work in both. He can claim a place of his own among the early Romantics. The rare atmosphere and tonality of his paintings, to which a deeper feeling was added in later years, will always assure him that place.

One can, as mentioned above, divide Corot's artistic life into two parts, although this does not do him full justice. His full powers may not be anticipated in the first phase, but conversely, in the second phase one can trace back his original genius. In his earlier, 'Italian' period, Corot did some striking works such as the *View of the Forum and the Colosseum*, now at the Louvre. He then painted mostly landscapes. The *View of Paris and St Cloud*, in the Musée Carnavalet, shows that his painting was becoming more and more harmonious and delicate. The output of his second stay in Italy would have been enough to fill a whole gallery.

He became more and more particular in his choice of subject. *Reminiscences of Albano, Reminiscences of the Borromean Isles*, were painted in Italy. at the same time that he drafted the *Flight into Egypt* for the chu.ch of Rosny. Back in France, he produced paintings such as the *Baptism of Christ* (a fresco for the church of St Nicholas du Chardonnet in Paris), *Mount Olive*, now at the Langres Museum, the *Bacchanale*, in Glasgow, the *Dance of the Nymphs* (Louvre), *Diana Bathing*, in Bordeaux, all of which show the fully matured master. Though 'officially' called a Romantic, Corot will always stand apart from any of the movements of the time. This is borne out by two of his late canvases, the *Belfrey of Douai* (1871) and *Sens Cathedral* (1875). A *Self-portrait* in the Uffizi, just one example among many, shows him as a master of portrait painting. His private life was exemplary. He was decent, kind and generous to his friends—among them Daumier and Millet. His art, in spite of some disappointments, brought him satisfaction. As he was modest in his needs, it was not difficult for him to find life rewarding. For the first painting of his which the French Government acquired (a landscape) he was paid 1,500 francs—a small sum even in 1846. However, they made him a

EDOUARD MANET: The Barricade (water-colour)

member of the Legion of Honour. Only after a posthumous exhibition of his works in 1896, did Corot's paintings begin to fetch higher prices, but by then he had been dead twenty years.

III

We are still concerned with the introduction to the art of the nineteenth century: it is difficult to put events into chronological order, because alongside the young painters whose work was to become the great event in the art history of the century, there still lived and worked older painters like Gros. Gros had trained a number of pupils, among them Charlet (1792—1845) and Raffet (1804—1860), whose pictures still echoed Napoleonic times. Here, too, Géricault (1791—1824) should be mentioned. He died young, leaving an important successor in Delacroix (1798—1863). Delacroix's choice of subject was usually historic and anecdotic. He brought about the disintegration of the sculptured form, which provoked Ingres to strong criticism.

Now we must talk about Ingres (1780—1867) himself. He was a pupil of David's, and was torn between Neoclassical and Romantic trends, vacillating between the *Moscardins* and the *Barbus*. The former were engrossed in mediaeval, the latter in primitive and antique, subjects. He went to Rome and took to imitating Raphael, for which he met with disapproval. He soon returned to his own style of painting, and produced canvases like the *Bather*, now in Bayonne, which had been on view in 1807. He became the most important—if a rather dogmatic—exponent of a strict classicism in painting, a master of pure, elegant, cold form. Colour was not his forte. Delacroix, twenty years his junior, said that Ingres' colours were like ' *de la nonpareille sur un gâteau bien cuit.*' In fact his *Apotheosis of Homer* (Louvre) has dirty yellow and at the same time shrieking colours, and therefore in spite of a certain amount of beauty, only disclosed at close inspection, cannot be accepted as a great painting. Ingres, when reproached for his choice of colour, maintained that a picture was well painted if it was well drawn. *The Apotheosis of Homer* is, however, according to our opinion not only badly painted but also untrue and tendentious. Among those doing homage to Homer he intentionally left out Goethe and Shakespeare because he thought them too romantic—this shows the hostility between the new trends of art and the old ones.

Géricault's work at first came under David's influence. From the *Raft of the Medusa* onwards, however, there is a new flow of movement and a new feeling in his pictures which points towards the future; but he has not yet completely broken away from the past. So the *Wounded Cuirassier*, in itself an important picture, is still conventionally drawn and still conventional in colour.

Ingres disapproved strongly of Delacroix: he calls him 'a sick Rubens, a neurotic Veronese'; but the young Delacroix, whose choice of colour was rich and whose technique was bold, prevailed over Ingres and asserted himself as the head of the new Romantic school. The *Death of Sardanapalus* and the *Massacre of Chios* show, as do other of his paintings, that he knew well how to deal with the iconographic contents of his pictures, how to group figures and how to establish a rapport between the individual groups.

Delacroix is a law unto himself—one would be at a loss to say who was his real teacher. What we know, however, is that he was influenced by Girodet (1767—1824), a painter whose choice of form was classical and whose spirit was Romantic. (The *Ossian Receiving the Generals of Napoleon*, at Malmaison, and his main work the *Deluge* are two examples.)

We now enter a phase of transition. The ageing Ingres still tries to hold out. 'The masters of this period,' says Reinach, 'still cling to the sculptured forms of David's school and its classical brush-work.' Yet Romanticism, mysticism, and sentimentalism force their way in; subjects become anecdotal; the figures of women and children take on a new grace; historic paintings such as Delaroche's and Couture's become characteristically large in size. They are mainly scenes from antiquity, such as Roman orgies, which cover up a style of uninhibited ostentation.

The mystics Flandrin, Cabanel and Bouguereau all show the stamp of Ingres' influence. This can be seen in Cabanel's *Birth of Venus* and in Bouguereau's somewhat syrupy but well-composed and well-drawn representations of religious subjects.

The democratic spirit which had become evident in one of Gros' paintings of Napoleon is carried on by his pupils (including the lithographers). Here Charlet and Raffet are once more called to mind; in

EDOUARD MANET: Portrait of Berthe Morisot (lithograph)

their battle scenes of the Revolution and the Empire they had focused interest on the ordinary soldier, his sufferings and his heroism, and not on the generals. Thus in *Napoleon at the Battle of Eylau*, Gros had placed an army surgeon in the centre of his canvas and had put Napoleon in the background. Meissonier (1815—1890), too, was attracted by military subjects. He painted small almost miniature-like canvases in the Dutch manner which at the time won him great fame. He was a pupil of Cogniet's and thus indirectly influenced by Charlet and Raffet. The critics valued Meissonier's *1814* above any Dutch or Italian painting of its kind and time.

It would be difficult to list in chronological order the works of the French artists who may be placed between Delacroix and Courbet. A few foreign painters, the Dutch Ary Scheffer and the Italian Giuseppe Palizzi, of the Barbizon School, worked at the same time. Giuseppe was a brother of Filippo Palizzi, a Neapolitan master of the nineteenth century, who was the more important of the two. Contemporary painting outside France will, in any case, have to be discussed later on, but I should like to mention briefly Gleyre, as his influence on the new movement and some of its exponents was considerable. Elie Delaunay (1828—1891), not to be confused with Robert Delaunay (1885—1941) who belongs to a later, quite different, school, was one of them. The painters of historic themes, Laurens, as well as Merson, Cormon and Duez, came under Gleyre's influence.

This introductory survey should not be concluded without mentioning the names of Decamps, Marilhat and Fromentin. Fromentin's paintings, mainly Arabic scenes, were somewhat superficial, but his critical work *Les Maîtres d'Autrefois* remains a source of information today. Decamps and Marilhat, both painters using a strong palette, were concerned chiefly with oriental subjects.

We have now come to the point when the Barbizon rebels had reached the peak of their campaign. Millet was soon to be passionately involved with them.

The question is, were these artists mainly engaged in their own personal rebellion based on the new revelations, the new Rights of Man, and the new intellectual concept ensuing from them? Or had a general fermentation also awoken the artistic conscience in other countries and given them the impetus for their strength and courage?

Similar experiments were being made in various places. Rousseau had tried to represent the image of Nature by strong light effects and little depth. Others, among them Ravier at Lyons, tried to do the same; yet he also imitated Delacroix's choice of colour without really being dependent on his way of painting in any other respect. So we see that feelers were put out in all directions, and the new movement spread like an epidemic. As the *genius loci* is different in different countries, so the results vary.

Mia Cinotti says: 'In the Germany of the years between 1830 and 1850 we found ourselves at the peak of the "Biedermeier" period, a charming, new anti-classical bourgeois style which preceded the March revolution of 1848. It was a meticulous art; it reproduced the human face, an interior or a landscape with equal love for intimate detail. Slightly apart from but of the same period as the Biedermeier artists was Caspar David Friedrich, with his faithfully yet poetically rendered landscapes. Later offshoots of German Romanticism were (the painters) Feuerbach and Hans von Marées. Feuerbach was academical and pretentious: Marées visionary and symbolical, reaching back for inspiration to the Nordic sagas and at the same time anticipating Gauguin. These artists and some of their followers, whose influence went far into the twentieth century, formed, one may say, the flank of the Munich school of realistic expression, of which Leibl and Thoma were the centre. Leibl and Thoma came under various influences: first Courbet's (but their line seems to be easier and clearer to follow), and then Menzel's, of the Berlin School, who with his vivid choice of colour came very near the French Impressionists.'

Mia Cinotti's short survey does not, of course, give a complete picture of anti-Neoclassical German painting, but it touches on essentials.

In this context, it is not inappropriate to talk further about Anselm Feuerbach (1829—1880), a lone wolf, who, though he had many teachers, was no one's pupil in particular. He founded no school of his own and therefore remains an isolated figure in German nineteenth century art. In 1942, Bodmer published in Italy the first volume of a detailed study of Feuerbach's work, with colour plates of the most important canvases.

Feuerbach's career was marked by defeat. Works of which he had great hopes were rejected by the critics and scorned by the public. He bore all the positive and negative characteristics of the German outlook; thus his life followed the pattern of many another German artist of the nineteenth century.

At a time when everyone was engrossed in colour problems, Feuerbach ignored the fact that historical painting was rich in 'period costume and beautiful settings'. He continued to strive for sculptured classical repose; he tried to evoke the 'spirit of antiquity' in his paintings, which were poor in theme but artistically ambitious.

Feuerbach's early youth was spent at Freiburg im Breisgau. He then attended the Düsseldorf Academy where he was a pupil of Schadow's. Sohn, Schirmer and Lessing were also his teachers but failed equally to influence him in his artistic aims. He then went to Munich—a reputation for precocious talent having preceded him there—and got into contact with Rahl, who was the first to have a lasting influence on his development. From Munich he went to Antwerp, from Antwerp to Paris, where he was carried along with the tide of French art and had at last the feeling of being on the right track. Many years later, when in Rome, he admitted to owing everything to the modern French painters of 1848, to Italy and to himself. In Paris he painted his first important canvas *Hafiz at the Well* which remained unsold.

He also lived for a time in Karlsruhe, where, among other pictures, he painted the *Death of Aretino*. In June, 1855, he went to Rome, where he was destined to remain. Ten years of hard work were to follow. Two versions of *Reminiscences of Tivoli*, *Plato's Symposium*, the *Judgment of Paris*, *Iphigenia*, *Medea*, and the *Battle of the Amazons* were some of the works of these years. In 1880 Feuerbach died of a stroke in Venice. He was buried at the Johannes Cemetery at Nuremberg, next to Dürer, Pirckheimer and Veit Stoss.

The most important of his Roman paintings, the *Medea*, hangs in the Munich Pinakothek. In it one feels the promise of a new monumental art whose development was cut short by Feuerbach's early death, leaving German painting the poorer for it.

Allgeyer wrote an excellent biography of this restless, individualistic man. It would, therefore, seem futile to dwell at such length on just another 'artist's life', but it is important to emphasise that at a time when German art, like art elsewhere, was torn by conflicting trends, Feuerbach went his own way and kept his independence.

Another movement in painting which was started at this time was the pre-Raphaelite Brotherhood, in England. Like other movements around 1848, it was in revolt against Neoclassical traditions.

The tenets of French painting, such as precedence of colour and atmosphere over form, and almost complete neglect of line, met, on the whole, with fellow-feeling in England, but were most readily accepted by the pre-Raphaelites, who turned them into a theatrical style which met with violent reactions.

Under the patronage of Ruskin and the leadership of Dante Gabriel Rossetti—both painter and poet, London-born but of Italian origin—a number of artists formed themselves into a brotherhood: Ford Madox Brown, Holman Hunt, Millais and Burne-Jones, among others. They tried to find in purity and simplicity, in neo-Gothic Romanticism and in Blake's visions an inspiration for new religious, social and moral subjects, and for the lasting form which they believed to be the attribute of art before Raphael had introduced formalism. Rossetti's *Paolo and Francesca* is one of the characteristic examples of this art. There was much talk of 'emotional truth' and revival, and the basis of the movement was the Italian Quattrocento. William Morris turned these principles to applied art, and his leadership contributed to the crafts movement.

Whichever way you look at it, the new style was a form of rebellion. There was rebellion everywhere; but the most interesting facet of it was the reaction of the public, and even more of the academicians, to the first manifestations of Romantic art.

IV

History of art, one would think, is built on firm ground and supported by generally acknowledged values. But in the nineteenth century even this stability was to be upset, so that Victor Hugo seems to have been right when calling it an independent century. Somarè, among others, made the intellectual and philosophical conditions—the soil, as it were, out of which grew the artistic revolution of the nineteenth century—the objects

EDOUARD MANET: Gipsies (engraving)

CLAUDE MONET: Women in a Garden (1866, Private Collection, Paris)

ALFRED SISLEY: The River Loing at Moret (Louvre, Paris)

CLAUDE MONET: Tulips in Holland (Louvre, Paris)

32

CLAUDE MONET: Boats at Argenteuil (Durand-Ruel Collection, Paris)

of thorough research. The effects of this revolution have not yet worn off. Somarè is quoted here because he is able to explain why the art of painting became unsure of itself, why its powers of perception became clouded and mistakes, the rule rather than the exception, were unfortunately discovered when it was too late.

'We should like to believe,' he says, 'in the existence of the absolute in the field of aesthetics, but this does not get us any further. It would not help matters either if we tried to cheat ourselves into the belief that painting can express the principles of such aesthetics visually and generally intelligibly. Artistic ideals vary from nation to nation, from individual to individual, and only the few who claim to have overcome by long and complicated processes of thought the chaotic relativity of taste have lifted the veil from that secret.' To this Somarè adds that the absolute in the field of aesthetics is by no means to be discovered with the eyes or the intellect, but that it is a distant goal towards which one must work one's way through uncertainty and contradictions which 'like leaves falling in the eternal autumn of history cover the laborious path of modern art'. One had, of course, been able to build up a standard for earlier art; there were the masterpieces of ancient art, of Early Christian art, and of the fifteenth-century Renaissance to establish a well-founded system of values. 'The spirit of the Greeks, of the Middle Ages and of the Renaissance, had, be it by interchange or by fusion, blended into a synthesis, which for centuries had been the basis of, and the pre-condition for, artistic creation and the intelligibility of art. Giotto, that austere and genuine exponent of Christian art, created frescoes whose figures together with the story they told were straightforward and easy to understand. The same applies to Masaccio in the fifteenth century and Giorgione in the sixteenth century. There were even then new movements in painting; yet however startling these may have been and however much they may have anticipated developments and general aesthetic awareness, they always went side by side with the public's awareness. The creative artist and his public were as one at that time. They both had the same ideals: conscious with the artist, unconscious with the public, but based on identical feelings.'

This happy sympathy between artist and public in former times shut out controversial criticism. 'Before, during and after the Renaissance and right up to the eighteenth century, potential difference of opinion on matters of taste and the theory of art, such as we know to have existed between Leonardo and Michelangelo, was a matter of personal controversy; it was not concerned with the essentials of art and did not touch on the naïve feelings of the public. Whether the argument was a heated one depended mostly on the disposition of the artists concerned and only rarely on a question of principle. With the end of the eighteenth century, however, this situation, which had brought about such long-lasting and perfect harmony, came to a sudden end; its basis, intellectual and emotional unity between the artist and his public, had gone. The cycle of antiquity (and its Renaissance revival) had fulfilled itself. The last remnants of it were the lovely gardens of the eighteenth century.' The new era was to be one of politics and philosophy. 'The Tree o Knowledge and its poisonous fruit now tempted minds which avidly searched for a new religion, new moral tenets and new aesthetics.' (This remark of Somarè's refers to the nineteenth century.) Similar ones have been made with reference to the movements of the twentieth century, and particularly to the period since 1945.

For centuries only art had generated art. From its lonely platform it had always reached out generously to be the giver; it had subordinated historic facts to its high aims; it had been the neutral guardian watching over that incorruptible treasure: the files of history. This independent development had now come to an end; art had become a matter for polemics. The intuitive foundations of artistic creation were forgotten or lost and with them the unity of mind. Tradition, 'that powerful mainspring of the past', from which epoch after epoch had gathered fresh strength, had lost its authority and become the mere custodian of various forms of artistic representation. These the art historians now painstakingly tried to classify, and they tried to derive new rules from them. These rules were to be followed willingly by the artists.

The academy and its canons had destroyed the close relationship between the artist and his public. From a historical plane it had been shifted to a cultural one and debased in the process. The return to the source of art became the question which preoccupied the artists of the day. The Romantics thought it to be inspiration, the Naturalists, reality. The situation was tense, antagonism and controversy unavoidable. Aesthetic balance was upset. Because of the contradictions between the many trends in art, the artists formed themselves into bigger or smaller groups, all hostile towards each other. This confused the public, and a rift ensued between their irresolute taste and the principles expressed by the few artists of genius who tried to bring art to its former uncontested high position. The critics who took the side of the public were unable to

EDOUARD MANET: La Toilette (water-colour)

34

ALFRED SISLEY: By the Banks of the Loing (etching)

resolve the conflict. The public and the artists now spoke a different language; the rift widened. One met generally with 'the annoying phenomenon of art being no longer grasped intuitively but, as it were, by delayed action.' Whereas before artists had expressed themselves in an exalted yet universally intelligible way, they now seemed inclined to use artificial, distinctly personal, exaggerated forms of expression.

The inheritance of the eighteenth century had been used up, and by the time the Neoclassical and academic periods of the first half of the nineteenth century had passed, the masters of that century met more or less with the same difficulties; the public was against them; they neither heeded them nor understood them. This public was so convinced that their 'way of seeing and judging things was the right one that it took decades to shake them out of the prejudices to which they adhered complacently.' Reports of the exhibitions of that time, the Paris Salons and the Italian *Permanenti* and *Promotrici*, were rife with scandal and full of misjudgments. The juries who organised these exhibitions consisted mostly of incompetent know-alls and pedantic dogmatists. 'They rejected the best and rewarded the worst.' The official criticism (and no other carried any weight) took great pains to explain to the visitors—who agreed with everything—that the good was bad and the bad was best. Thus Courbet's paintings were quite often rejected by the Salons.

V

The fixed points around which revolved the creed of the Romantic artists were of a philosophic, aesthetic and technical nature. And although one can talk about communal features in an artistic movement, the fact still remains that a work of art will always be the independent act of the individual artist.

The artist is free. Man takes pride of place in artistic creation; Nature is not made to look theatrical, and the aim is to represent the real image of life. The fleeting moment must be caught. Technique should be free, as the artist expresses, in his work, himself, his feelings and his intentions. There are some artists who

BERTHE MORISOT: Girls Drawing (engraving)

put themselves too much in the foreground; others are more modest. Some are fascinated by the spectacle of Nature; others explore a character in a portrait, and still others try to depict social problems.

The freedom of the artist is based on the liberation of man; and the awareness of this liberation we find first and foremost in Millet's work.

Jean François Millet (1814—1875) was faithful to Barbizon, where he died, at the age of sixty. He is, like Corot, though in a different way, one of the precursors of Impressionism. At the beginning of his career —from 1840 on, he was sending pictures to the Salons which were mostly rejected by the selection committees— his painting showed the new attitudes; later on, once more subject took precedence over technique for him. He was soon forgotten and only recently has his name been reinstated. Millet was a painter who provoked a lot of controversy and was even rejected by critics of a certain modern tendency.

Putting his personal success into the balance, one comes to the conclusion that he was a good painter in his early career and a bad one towards the end. He was the son of peasants and was born at Gruchy, a village near Cherbourg and Gréville. He won a scholarship which enabled him to go to Paris, to the Ecole des Beaux-Arts. Later, Delaroche became his teacher. He learned the craft of painting from him, but his love of it was inspired by frequent visits to the Louvre. The Louvre was really his academy and his university; observing Nature did the rest. His temperament, however, was largely responsible for all that was novel in the subject matter of his pictures. This new approach to content roused—at least for some years—general interest, and even won him fame with part of the public. Later on it was to make life difficult for him and to turn him into a recluse. Victor Hugo had this to say: 'The revolution created two myths—one artistic and spiritual as expressed by Romanticism, and one political as expressed by Socialism.' This latter, as the poet remarks, *se prête à tant d'interprétations différentes*. Thanks to his love of nature, Millet was the first to move away more and more noticeably from the pattern of Romanticism. The most striking feature of his work was the deeply emotional way in which he represented the peasantry. The subject in itself was such as to provoke heated controversy. Even his merits as a portrait painter could not alter that; especially as in his portraiture he was inclined to express passion above anything else. 'Van Gogh admired him and made use of some of his motifs, expressing them, it is true, in quite a different manner.'

How can Millet be reproached from the critics' point of view? His genre studies, as is generally agreed, are as touching and unforgettable as folk tales. His drawing shows talent and is always carefully and well done. His choice of colour, even if somewhat conventional and unimaginative, does not offend the eye. His sympathy for the peasants was true, and, coming himself from peasant stock, he was intimately familiar with their way of life. He must also be credited with true religious feeling, a liberal social outlook and a lyrical sentiment which at times he was able to convey in his paintings. Why, then, is he denied the reputation of a great artist? Venturi has analysed Millet's most famous canvas the *Angelus*. It shows two peasants, a man and a woman, at the end of their day's work deep in prayer; the figures are set in the foreground of a wide plain. In the sky the light is still strong; on the ground it is muted. Reminiscences of a personal experience gave this picture a special, intimate note. In what way does Venturi find fault with it? 'Millet is unable to convince us that this picture is a work of art. His love for his peasant friends causes him to underline their piety, their sincerity and their purity. He wants to convince the French public of the rights of the proletarian... from a moral and social point of view this is justified, but in the process of representing it his picture takes on the form of a plea for vindication; not a way in which a work of art should impress the viewer. Millet's scene must be called sentimental: true feeling manifests itself by natural approach to reality; sentimentality tries to convince the onlooker by sentiment which kills what genuine feeling there may have been... If we claim that the first essential of art is sincerity we must be clear of its meaning in art history. Millet is perfectly sincere in his convictions in the same way that most people who claim to be sincere are convinced, but this is not enough. Theories have never created a work of art. The moral attitude conveyed by Millet's paintings is sincere, but again this does not of itself make a work of art, as sincerity of thought and endeavour are not by any means identical with art. By asking that an artist should be sincere we in fact ask that he should be "spontaneous". In the process of artistic creation perceptiveness and imagination should never be inhibited by intellectual or moral concepts, however true these may have appeared to the artist. Artistic creation should flow as naturally as a tree grows or a flower opens. Spontaneity certainly implies sincerity but does not completely cover it.' Arguments, as we see, become more and more complex.

After analysing his paintings we can say this of Millet: he stands between the Barbizon School and the Realists. He had the same love for the woods of Fontainebleau as had Théodore Rousseau, but his peasant paintings, his portraits and his technique seem nearer to Courbet. His sad life is not unlike Daumier's.

Gustave Courbet (1819—1877) came from Ornans in the Franche Comté. He was largely self-taught, and though he was drawn to painting at the age of twenty he seldom attended classes at Steuben's studio in Paris. Hesse admitted that Courbet only became his pupil in order that he might help him to be accepted at the Salon of 1844. There the young painter exhibited his *Self-portrait with a Black Dog*, which had been painted some time before. This work, with its personal note, shows the future talent of the painter; but at that time Courbet still had a love for the Romantic, which one sees in his pictures *All Hallows Eve, Lovers in the Country* and in the *Guitarist*, painted in 1845. During this period he often went to the Louvre and felt more and more attracted by the Spanish and Dutch masters.

Political happenings at that time had an influence on the organisation of art exhibitions in the traditional Salon. After the fall of Louis Philippe, Louis Napoleon (later Napoleon III) was elected President of the French Republic.

Because of these events there was no selection committee at the Salon of 1848. This was a chance for artists whose work was not of a tested and approved standard and which also showed marked independence. The exhibition passed unnoticed and undiscussed. The pictures were rejected in bulk, and nobody even took the trouble to notice Courbet's *Cellist*, or his other paintings and many drawings that were on show.

In the following year the committee sat again, and therefore Courbet had only two works on show: *After Dinner at Ornans* and *Man with a Leather Belt*; other important canvases of his were rejected. Cogniat has this to say about it: 'It really seems that Courbet wanted to be a painter in order to give material reality to the pleasure he took in looking at Nature. He spread colour on to the canvas with the essential joy of a gourmand; the foliage of a forest, the water of a cascade, are means of seizing throbbing life; even Courbet's political attitudes were a kind of physical expansion—a means of life and freedom and not a philosophical creed thought out with man's destiny in mind... his first canvases show distinct signs of Romanticism, and the Realism of his later work was not a denial of it but rather a logical development, a sort of violent affirmation of his early passion for life. Because of the titles of these paintings, Courbet's contemporaries had serious reservations about his work.'

There Cogniat has in mind such pictures as the *Burial at Ornans*, the *Stonebreakers, Bonjour Monsieur Courbet* and the *Bathers*, all painted within a year or two of 1848. Many of his pictures provoked the indignation of the Court (it was the time of the Second Empire) and the public. The figures in the *Burial* were portraits of living people. Criticism was violent. Jacques Combé remarked that the public seemed hardly able to bear the fact that anybody should represent human beings and life in such an undisguised way. One must consider that the favourite painters at that time were still Ingres, Delacroix, Delaroche, Horace Vernet and Couture; but even they were sometimes criticised. Apart from all this, Courbet's republican ideas were well known, and the mere fact that he represented people of the lower classes at work was provoking. To the *Burial* a special story is attached, as Courbet himself said, in a letter quoted by Hartlaub: 'The people who posed for me were: the Mayor (of Ornans), weighing four hundred pounds; the Priest; a justice of the peace—the man who carried the crucifix; two old people of the time of the Revolution in the dress of that time; a dog; a corpse and its bearers; the sextons, one of whom had a bright red fat nose, five inches long; my own sisters; some other women, etc.' This picture with its crowd is now at the Louvre. Courbet continues: 'I hoped I could have done without the two choristers, but this was impossible because they were most annoyed that they were the only ones I had left out of the congregation. They protested, saying that they had never done me any harm...'

So Courbet had to include the two singers, 'on a canvas twenty feet long and ten feet wide which was peopled by fifty life-size figures'.

In the violent polemics which raged round Courbet his defenders were, apart from the unerring Baudelaire, Thoré-Burger, Champfleury and Daumier. 'Out of these controversies, between 1850 and 1855, Realism was born, and Courbet found himself at the head of the new school.'

ALBERT MARQUET: Study from the nude

'The label of Realist was connected with my name in the same way as that of Romantic was with the men of 1830. Words never give the real meaning of things. If this were not so, works of art would be redundant. Without trying to find out whether the label is really the right one—I hope nobody is asked to understand it completely—I restrict myself to some explanations in order to avoid any misunderstanding... (Courbet was a first-class dialectic. He had been a student at the Besançon Lycée, and before that had attended a Seminary)... I studied the art of classical antiquity and of modern times, avoiding a system which would tie me to preconceived ideas. I did not want to be committed to either of these epochs and even less was the sterile slogan of art for art's sake my aim. No! What I really wanted was to create an artistic awareness which would be independent of my own person; I started on this with a comprehensive knowledge of tradition. My precepts were: to know in order to be able to create; to be capable of rendering the ethics, the thoughts and the events of my era such as I understood them; in short I did not want only to be a painter but wanted also to be a human being. To create living art was my aim.'

Tempers rose when Courbet exhibited the *Bathers*, the *Wrestlers* and the *Spinning-woman Asleep*. Bruyas, however, acquired two of these pictures and invited the painter to settle at Montpellier. There he created new works: the *Encounter*, some landscapes and some seascapes. His technique became more and more vigorous, and he brightened his palette. The *Studio* and other older, not yet exhibited, works were rejected by the Committee of the Exposition Universelle of 1855. Thereupon Courbet put on his own show in a hut opposite the main entrance of the exhibition.

Though immediate success was denied him, the number of his admirers increased from then on. He worked in Paris (*Young Girls on the Banks of the Seine* [1857], *Fighting Stags, Stag Drinking, Horses in Hiding* [1861]); he travelled to the Franche Comté, to Frankfurt, to Antwerp and Le Havre. At Saintes he met Corot for the first time. He continued to paint. At the Salon of 1863 *Return from the Conference* was rejected because of its anti-clerical character. That did not worry him; he painted *Venus and Psyche* to try his hand at nudes, a *Portrait of Prud'hon* and the *Woman with Parrot*. In 1865, at the same time as the Exposition Universelle, he put on a one man show of a hundred paintings. The success of this was moderate, but the great acclaim accorded his Munich show of 1869 compensated him. Then came the Franco-Prussian war, the French defeat, the Commune and the new French Republic which was bound to disappoint him.

Courbet felt himself more and more a revolutionary and a *citoyen*. He was a member of the Commune and asked the new government to destroy the Vendôme Column, which was faced with the bronze of twelve hundred cannons looted by Napoleon in 1805, and the top of which was crowned by a statue of the Emperor. This column, the symbol of bygone tyranny, was not destroyed by command of the government but by the rage of the people. Courbet was made responsible for this act of vandalism and was sentenced to six months' imprisonment. He spent this time at Sainte-Pélagie, where he painted still-lifes (1871). Meissonier, who was very influential, rejected them at the Salon of the following year. In addition to this the President of the Republic, MacMahon, wanted to re-erect the column and Courbet was asked to pay for that.

Courbet was ruined. His resistance was broken. He found neither rest nor a place to live in France. The last seven years of his gallant life he spent in Vevey (La Tour de Peilz) in Switzerland.

Baudelaire, who admired him as the great master he was, said about Courbet that 'his thoroughness was constructive and fostered high epic qualities'—certainly resounding, if not very clearly defined, praise. Courbet, one might say, painted in a broad technique. He mixed and spread his tones generously, put colours on canvas with a palette knife, used ordinary brushes instead of painters' brushes. With this he achieved luminous colour effects on dark ground. One should also say that he put his whole art into the service of his social concepts, as, for instance, in the *Stonebreakers*. This was painted from real life; Courbet invited the men to his studio, talked to them and then glorified their misery and toil in a picture that became a flaming protest to lack of human sympathy.

We should not forget that Courbet was a revolutionary in politics and a herald of high ideals. Yet he did not wish to be labelled an idealist...

They were, however, all idealists then, annoyed and irritated as they may have been to be called that; even the younger generation of painters who were born between 1830 and 1840 and were the real protagonists of Impressionism: Pissarro, Degas, Monet, Renoir and Sisley, to mention only a few; and, of course,

GUSTAVE COURBET: Young Girls on the Banks of the Seine (Petit Palais, Paris)

CAMILLE PISSARRO: Landscape near Eragny (1895, Louvre, Paris)

CAMILLE PISSARRO: The Herdswoman (1880, Louvre, Paris)

ALFRED SISLEY: Floods at Port Marly (1876, Louvre, Paris)

EDGAR DEGAS: Portrait of a Woman (pastel and water-colour)

ROGER DE LA FRESNAYE: Study. Drawing

Cézanne, whose work was to open a door to the future, and Manet who stood at the beginning of the movement but was never quite of it.

Edouard Manet (1832—1883) never managed to be completely in tune with his friends of the Café Guerbois, though he was stimulated early on to use bright colours and a delicate technique by Eugène Boudin (1824—1898), and even more so by the Dutch painter Jongkind (1819—1891).

He did not blindly follow this technique of bright colours, nor did he ever completely master it. His outdoor painting did not prevent him from painting also from imagination. He 'masters at the same time the traditional and the contemporary, with all that it implies.' In this lies the secret of the monumental design, the shimmering atmosphere and the artistic quality of his canvases. Manet came from the upper-middle classes and should by rights have become a lawyer or an admiral; his interest in painting, however, led him to become a pupil of Couture, who had also been Feuerbach's teacher. His opinion very often differed from his academic master's, whose influence, however, prevented him from following his own impulses in an unbridled way: thus, for instance, he went on using dark colours for quite some time, until at last

Mary Cassatt: Mother and Child (engraving)

he broke away from his teacher and sent the *Absinthe Drinker* to the Salon of 1859 where, needless to say, it was rejected.

The *Absinthe Drinker* reminded his contemporaries of Goya. Goya's Spanish influence on Manet can be explained by Manet's frequent visits to the Louvre and later by his journey to Spain, and is to be found in the *Guitarist*, the *Portrait of Lola* and the *Old Musician*. Before going to Spain in 1865, Manet had been to Austria and Germany, and to Holland and Italy. Wherever he went he remained the typical *boulevardier*: witty and unprejudiced. He had to be fairly independent to send to the Salon of 1863 a picture like the *Déjeuner sur l'Herbe*, now at the Louvre, but then relentlessly rejected by the Committee—whereupon Manet promptly showed it at the Salon des Refusés. Considering the attitude of Parisian society at that time, the scandal it provoked is not really surprising. Fresh air blows through that landscape, and this is its extra-ordinary merit. What sort of lamdscape is it? A glade with two young men, rather heavily dressed for a meal in the open air, sitting on the ground—young men like *ceux qu'on rencontre dans la vie*, or in the street or on the boulevard. It is well known that these two male figures are portraits of Eugène Manet, the painter's brother, and Ferdinand Leenhoff, his future brother-in-law. It would be just another family group had Manet not chosen to put the elegantly unperturbed, seated figure of a young woman in the nude (inci-dentally this was his model Victorine Meurend) into the foreground; and in the background is a scantily clothed woman who seems to be undressing for a bathe in the nearby pond.

The year was 1863; the time, the Second Empire. There is no immodesty in this peaceful scene as we see it; but how, at that time, did one make sense of a naked woman in a wood together with two clothed young men? She is by no means provocative—less so than the other, half-dressed, figure; but there she sits, unclothed in the woods.

The Paris bourgeoisie was seething with rage. 'What desecration of Art!' clamoured the high priests. And if we think of the scandal about *Madame Bovary* we need not be surprised at the outcry.

And yet many pictures of Venus, Juno and Diana had been exhibited at the various Salons which were, if possible, more in the nude than Mademoiselle Victorine (and not as well painted). What really upset the public was the freedom of the open-air setting and the portraiture of the models. These were portraits, and therefore these people must have sat for them—even the unclothed Victorine. This was what they reproached Manet with, but it would have been more to the point had they reproached him with borrowing the elements of his composition from Raphael's *Judgment of Paris* or even more so from Giorgione's *Concert*. And could one not say of *Olympia* (1865) that the horizontal figure recalled Goya's *Maja Desnuda?* (The colouring of the skin and of the ornaments on the material and the flowers, it is true, is of a delicacy all its own.) Or had Manet been influenced by Titian's *Venus?*

In the same year (1865) Manet, who by then had Degas' support, joined Bazille, Renoir, Sisley, Pissarro, Cézanne and Monet.

Manet went on working. As has been said before, he used bright colours and handled black tones with real taste and rare elegance.

Of Manet's works which are, each for a different reason, particularly remarkable and typical, I should like to mention the following: *Boy with a Sword* (1861, Metropolitan Museum of Art, New York), the *Old Musician* (1861, also at the Metropolitan Museum), *Concert in the Tuileries* (1862, National Gallery, London), the *Fifer* (1866, Louvre), the *Execution of Maximilian*, reminiscent of Goya (1867, National Gallery, London), *Breakfast in the Studio* (1868, Bavarian State Gallery, Munich), the *Lecture* (1868, Louvre), *Portrait of Emile Zola* (Louvre), painted in homage to the writer who supported Manet and his courageous friends and their works in their battle with a public opinion which had been quite unprepared for their new approach.

In the Mendelsohn Collection in Berlin, later works of Manet's such as the *Harbour of Bordeaux* can be seen; they have the same vigorous colouring which lifts the whole picture on to a higher spiritual plane. To these we should like to add the *Washing Day* (Cassirer Collection, Amsterdam), the *Waitress* (National Gallery, London). The ostracised and rehabilitated *Olympia* now hangs at the Louvre as does the *Déjeuner*. There we also find, apart from the *Portrait of Emile Zola*, two other portraits by Manet which should be mentioned for their technique, their purity of colour and their psychological representation: the *Portrait of Irma Brunner* and that of *Eva Gonzales*. There are some other works of Manet's which could be looked upon

WASSILY KANDINSKY: Drawing

PIERRE AUGUSTE RENOIR: Portrait of a Young Girl (1885, Private Collection, Paris)

as portraits, though the painter doesn't call them that: *Blonde with Bare Breast*, *Woman in a Garden*, and others. Manet was fortunate enough to receive in his lifetime the honours which came to him and to his work. At that time the Cross of the Legion of Honour was not as common as it was to become later on, and even a revolutionary like Manet accepted it gladly. Also, Manet was constantly divided between views and aspirations which were opposed to each other. In one way he was the true revolutionary who turned the taste of Parisian society upside down, provoking hostility and fierce controversy everywhere, finding friends only among the few great minds of the time. In another way his upper middle-class upbringing and tastes prevented him from standing openly by his young admirers who, under his flag, declared war on the Salons. Manet never intended to break away from the bourgeois society of the Second Empire; yet in his works he constantly gave offence to this very society. That he was made an officer of the Legion of Honour did not make any difference to that. He remained a solitary, controversial figure among the artists of the day.

At the same time other artists went on painting in the manner of Corot and Millet. The most important of this second group were Français, Harpignies, Cazin and Pointelin. Reinach sees in Jules Breton, who, like Millet, painted peasants and rustic scenes, an artist who was striving to reconcile poetic and realistic representation without sacrificing beauty and grace. By 1855, academicism and the calligraphic manner had run its course, and Romanticism was faced with the reaction against Realism and Naturalism as represented by Courbet and Manet respectively.

Among the artists who painted the human figure *en plein air* was Bastien-Lepage (1848—1884). *Plein air* painting originated with Manet, whose technique was to use pure colours, one superimposed on the other. In this he was followed by Pissarro, Sisley and Monet.

PABLO PICASSO: Study. Drawing

With Claude Monet (1840—1926) we are entering the period of Impressionism proper. He came of bourgeois stock and was a pupil of Gleyre's, as were Renoir, Sisley and some of the other innovators; he, however, soon broke away from Gleyre. It was not Gleyre who influenced Monet, but Constant Troyon. Troyon had based his work on Rembrandt, Potter and Cuyp and was so orthodox a painter that none of his pictures were refused at the Salons between 1833 and 1859; he was even accepted by the Academy in Amsterdam. But Troyon studied Nature (he painted cattle and horses) and had a fine perception of it and a facile and fresh way of rendering it. At the early age of sixteen, at Le Havre, Monet was aware of the charm of Troyon's canvases; at that time he exhibited there together with Boudin.

Gleyre did not exercise great influence over the unruly crowd of pupils who frequented his studio. They all painted with Courbet in mind and were often seen at the Café Guerbois, their real academy, their parliament and the platform of the new movement. Monet was even at that early stage an eminent figure in the young circle round Manet; the reaction to his work, however, was not yet very great. With the *Seine at Honfleur*, he was first admitted to the Salon of 1865. In the following years, with *Saint Germain in Auxerre*, *Portrait of Camilla* (his first wife), the first *Breakfast* (a harmonious interior in discreet colours) and particularly with the second *Breakfast* (in *plein air*), he pushed his obsession with reality to its limits, and by the most deliberate use of light effects precipitated the revolution against academic conventions.

At that time France was at war (1870). The group of artists dispersed. Bazille, of whom we will talk later, served with the Zouaves and was killed in battle; Monet and some of the others went to London and applied themselves there to the study of Hogarth and, to a greater extent, of Turner.

After their return to France the fight began. The artists now refused to satisfy current public taste and the fashion of the day; they would not work to set themes nor would they use obsolete techniques. '*Désormais l'artiste donne la priorité à sa propre émotion et rend le public témoin de son état d'âme.*' The work of art became highly personal, and Monet subscribed to this with a frankness that seemed unacceptable.

Whatever the artists may have had to say, the selection committees of the Salons rejected them all on principle: Pissarro and Sisley, Renoir, Cézanne and Degas.

Confronted with this untenable situation, the avant-garde artists made a *sortie* from the Café Guerbois. They formed themselves into the *Société Anonyme des Peintres, Sculpteurs et Graveurs* and decided to organise their own independent shows. But where? Without delay 35 Boulevard des Capucines, a photographer's studio, was put at their disposal. We would in any case be indebted to Nadar—that was the photographer's name—for helping these artists, but what made it a real act of Christian charity was that these painters had always shown a marked contempt for photographic reality. On April 15th, 1874, the first exhibition *chez Nadar* was opened in these rooms. Monet showed a picture called *Impression—Soleil Levant*. Treating the title ironically, a journalist, Louis Leroy, called Monet an Impressionist and his painting Impressionism. This nickname stuck; the new movement was christened. Apart from Monet's distinctly polemic works, his paintings are never optical illusions but are expressions of the spirit or are a lyrical moment captured. The key to Monet's personality is that he always saw the miracle of Nature, and by his skill he managed to make the miracle seem natural; and because he aspired to render the miraculous, 'he invented Impressionistic technique' (Venturi). He did this to express the vibration of all things alive. Venturi adds: 'This was rather a bold innovation which had become necessary to him because of his reaction to the traditional way of painting and because of his unshakable belief in his own way of expressing things.'

Monet was a fighter; he was not to be defeated by the critics. Not even the precarious financial position to which the hostility of the public and the indifferent attitude of the art dealers had reduced him could change that. The field of his activities widened; he painted the *Bridge Over the Seine at Argenteuil* (1874), the *Seine* (1879), *Fishermen on the Seine* (1881), various views of *Rouen Cathedral* (1892-5), views of *London* (1905), of *Venice* (1908) and the luminous *Water-lilies*, among others. His main concern was to show shimmering light.

One day in 1883 he was forced to ask Manet 'to find somebody who could buy ten or twenty of my pictures according to his own choice for a hundred francs apiece.' Manet went in search of a friend who would be willing to match the five hundred francs which he had contributed out of his own pocket. They found such a man, and they planned to make this leading French Impressionist believe that a dealer had been prepared to pay the requested price for ten of his paintings.

EDOUARD MANET: The Old Musician (detail) (1862, National Gallery of Art, Washington)

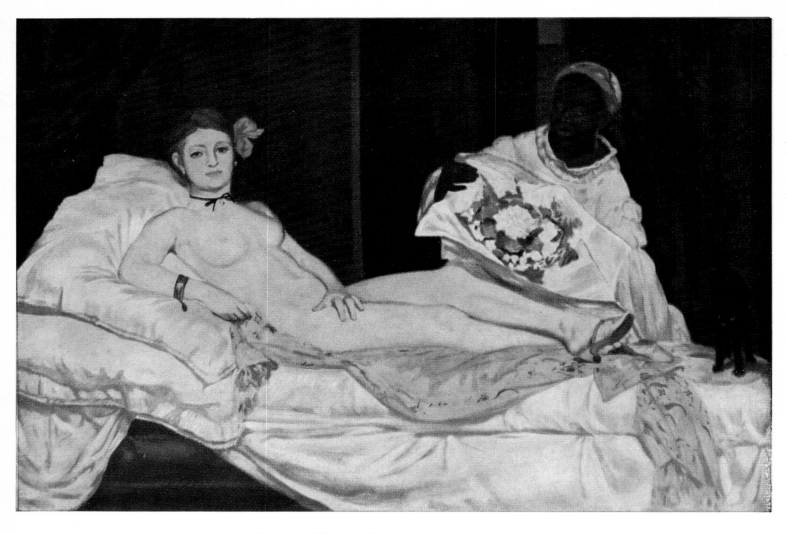

EDOUARD MANET: Olympia (1863, Louvre, Paris)

Edouard Manet: Le Déjeuner sur l'Herbe (1863, Louvre, Paris)

ALFRED SISLEY: La Grande Jatte (1873, Louvre, Paris)

EDGAR DEGAS: Dancers in the
Wings (detail) (1880, Collection
of Mrs Edward Jones, New York)

The artists of that circle appreciated each other and helped each other. Monet, too, bought 'in the name of some subscribers' Manet's *Olympia* and sent the picture to the then Minister of Education and later President of the Republic, Clément Armand Fallières. 'Take this picture,' he said. 'It is our wish that it should hang in the Louvre.' Thus he fought and won Manet's battle.

His own struggle went on. 'The effect of light on water and the landscape is becoming an obsession with me. It is too much for my reduced strength, and yet I want to represent what I feel. I have destroyed part of my work, but something will emerge from all this toil.'

What emerged was the final victory and apotheosis of Impressionism, the formidable, far-reaching, convincing power of the movement which, as time went on, was able to get its message through to the masses.

VI

The word Impressionism is more an art historian's label than a definition. We know by now that apart from those forerunners already mentioned, Manet and Monet were the exponents of the movement; and we will soon hear more about their fellow-painters Sisley, Pissarro, Degas and Renoir.

It does not seem easy, however, to translate a definition into a brief, appropriate formula. We have to fall back on manuals to define that 'vast, new movement which, in the first half of the century, was at work in France among a group of painters called Impressionists.' The profound revolution brought about by these artists covered the whole field of painting both in concept and technique. They were Naturalists in as much as they did not recognise any other principle but Nature. Abstract Nature was not the object of their exploration, but Nature as revealed by sensual perception: 'Nature quasi-representing a mood.' They faced her free of any preconceived ideological prejudices and of intellectual or moral inhibitions, determined to extract

PIERRE AUGUSTE RENOIR: Girls Bathing (etching)

PIERRE AUGUSTE RENOIR: Head of a Girl (pencil drawing)

from her only such visual elements of beauty as are translatable into colour and form. Therefore they gave their attention to the visual world in general without choosing any particular subject to begin with. They preferred to paint in the open air: landscapes, views, scenes of everyday life, portraits, still-lifes—always trying to grasp such elements as can be rendered in painting and which, if realised, achieve an unmistakable transfiguration of reality. These basic principles of theirs necessarily involved a new technique which they invented and applied. They felt that the different schools of painting at that time, be they Neoclassical, Romantic or Realist, were but convenient abstractions. To be freed of conventions of any sort they set up new principles based on nature and on their own perceptions. They first established the fact that 'their own visual sensations were akin to the shimmering of light,' that the form and colour of objects were not perceived in even, clearly defined lines, but were in constant pulsation; that in Nature the academic chiaroscuro did not exist; that 'there were colour contrasts only and no neutral shades,' that the play of light brightened colour, and that in order to achieve a similar brightness on the canvas colours must be separated.

All Impressionists, allowing for the individual temperament of each artist, worked more or less on these principles. 'The affinity of their personal, and generally speaking, also of their social position, was strengthened by constant contact and firm friendship between them—by which they built up a united front against the hostility they met with.' Until 1886, collective exhibitions were held periodically in Paris. From that year onwards the individual members of the circle began to experiment on their own. From Monet, who availed himself of the scientific theory of complementary colours to achieve his impalpable atmospheric effects—which led Pissarro and Seurat to Divisionism—to Cézanne, who tried by the critical analysis of impressions and their integration in a higher, as it were metaphysical, order, these men attempted to arrive at an absolute yet impermanent form.

Almost the whole of Western painting at the end of the nineteenth century came under Impressionist influence.

The importance of Impressionist painting is based on the fact that the Impressionists succeeded in bringing Nature and imagination into full harmony. As descendants of a middle-class society at the height of its cultural achievements, they reflected the optimistic, mobile, realistic spirit of that society.

One must remember, however, that the main characteristic of Impressionism was that it was a spiritual attitude towards light. This light radiates abundantly from the audacious colours of the magnificent paintings which were later recognised as the masterpieces of Impressionism. This light is never static; it changes every moment, alters the contours of objects and thus resembles the workings of the mind.

The Impressionist movement had so much vitality that at the moment of its decline it was able to generate its own successors. They were the Neo-Impressionists, Fauves, Cubists, Futurists and Expressionists. Today they all belong to history.

At the peak of French *plein-air* painting there were artists to whom the public (and the critics) did not grant the title of master; yet they were the backbone of the period. To this group belonged Camille Pissarro (1831—1903), and other painters of the Café Guerbois circle.

Pissarro was born in St Thomas in the Antilles. In 1852, he went to live in Venezuela. The Dutch painter Fritz Melbye predicted a great future for him as an artist. Pissarro came to Paris in 1855, and there he met Corot. In 1857 he made the acquaintance of Manet. Corot was at that time sixty, Manet just under seventeen. So Pissarro's first attempts at painting oscillate between these two extremes. He was the son of a Portuguese Jew who had become a naturalised French subject. He had crossed the Atlantic three times, and had had all sorts of experiences in life including some in business. Though he felt drawn to Millet, he was swept along in the wake of Monet. His rather poetic nature prevented him from adhering to a strict technique; his artistic eye was not as perceptive as Monet's, yet his works suggest a certain element of dramatic mood.

Pissarro, as was only to be expected, also took part in the revolt against studio painting; he painted black shadows which in reality are not the counterpart of light, and yet he was a painter who was able to lay on colour broadly and with consummate skill. Above all his colour was nearly always of incomparable luminosity; that was why he could succeed at the exhibitions of 1874, 1876 and 1877 at Nadar's. Before that he had shown at the Salon des Refusés. He was an industrious painter; one could not begin to enumerate his many drawings which show that he was also an Impressionist with his pencil. Of his paintings we would like to

PIERRE AUGUSTE RENOIR: Woman with a Muff (pen-and-ink drawing)

mention the following: *Arrival at the Village* (1872, Louvre), *Road to Louveciennes* (1870, Louvre), the *Oise at Pontoise* (1873, Louvre), the *Kitchen Garden* (1871, Louvre), *Cow Grazing* (Louvre) and *Portrait of a Peasant Woman* (National Gallery, Washington). All these works and many others show the coherence of his artistic principles. Unfortunately, this did not make him much money. His financial difficulties really began when, after moving from Montmorency to Lavarenne-Saint Hilaire, he married. Other moves followed: to Pontoise, to Louveciennes, etc., during which time he had seven children. But his paintings still did not pay. When, in 1871, the Franco-Prussian war broke out, he went to London, as did other French artists. On his return he found his studio ransacked, and it is believed that several hundred pictures were destroyed or damaged. With characteristic speed and versatility, he painted new pictures and valiantly faced the indifference and hostility of public and officials. Even as late as 1890-1895 Impressionism was practically ostracised. The sensational Caillebotte affair (1893) shows only too clearly the unfortunate attitude of official France. Caillebotte, a rich man, a generous artist and a friend of many artists, had gradually acquired a great number of paintings from his colleagues. On his death he left seventy-seven pictures to the Musée Luxembourg. In spite of the intervention of Degas—who was the executor of his will and who tried to persuade the government to accept them—thirty-two of the paintings were rejected: three Cézannes, three Degas, two Manets, eight Monets and eleven Pissarros! This seems hard to believe today.

In the end Pissarro managed to achieve a certain financial affluence; by that time, however, his eyesight had become poor, and this prevented him from painting in the open air. His last years were rather pathetic. He used to climb up to the upper floors of various Parisian houses inhabited by friends or strangers—even to hotels—and to paint behind closed windows what he could see of the Tuileries Gardens, the Avenue de l'Opéra and the bridges over the Seine. These canvases were mainly of winter scenes seen in more or less vertical perspective, i.e. painted from above looking down. He died in Paris in 1903.

Alfred Sisley's (1839—1899) experiences as an artist were similar to those of Pissarro. Pissarro had attached himself to Monet, and Sisley now attached himself to Pissarro, Monet and the others. Together they formed a united group which represented the most important artistic trends of the second half of the nineteenth century.

Here we should like once more to point out the connections between artistic development and political and social conditions at that time. The mature years of the most important exponents of Impressionism coincide with the date of the Battle of Sedan, the Commune and the social experiments of the Third Republic. These experiments, as Dino Formaggio writes, are of paramount importance to the development of the artists: ' In the years after 1870 France was under the depressing influence of a lost war. This defeat also seems to have had cultural repercussions and to have led to the decadent movements which prevailed towards the end of the century.' The highly taxed social conscience of the whole nation, which had been solidly based on national and political tenets and had been the mainstay of Courbet's artistic and political activities, left the outgoing century facing almost insoluble problems; these were more of an ethical than an artistic nature. Courbet's career ended, as we said before, in exile. The crisis over the European balance of power ended with Prussia's (and Bismarck's) victory; and as in every other post-war period, brute force seemed to have taken supremacy over reason. Confronted with a revaluation of all standards, ' the artist often chooses isolation, shielding behind his art,' and thus tries to find security against the disappointment and possible collapse of his humane ideals.' Now the Romantic slogan of *l'art pour l'art* takes on a new historic significance and becomes a new tragic truth. So we find in the very splendour of Impressionism the portentous turning-point of modern art with its as yet unforseeable consequences. It is the conflict of an art torn between the exigencies of reality and the temptation of shunning it.

Sisley, also a pupil of Gleyre's, joined his studio at the age of twenty-three. There he met Bazille, Monet and Renoir, and was, like them, attracted by the magic of Fontainebleau. The Barbizon School, it is true, had ceased to exist, but the countryside still held its old charm. Sisley secured a place of honour for himself in the Impressionist Group only after his death. Being of English extraction and well off into the bargain, he met with the diffidence of his colleages, who looked upon him as an amateur. To be acknowledged as an artist he had to meet with financial ruin, caused by the 1870-71 war, and had to paint for his living as did his fellow artists. He went to Normandy several times (1895), to the Welsh coast (1897) and to Moret-sur-

Loing, where he died after a life devoted to his work. Only then did his paintings, with their calm atmosphere, their delicate light effects and their lyrical appeal find recognition by the public. Among these paintings are: *Marly—the Canal*, (1872, Louvre), *Small Square at Argenteuil* (1872, Louvre), *Boats at the Lock of Bougival* (1873, Louvre), *Seine Landscape* (1875, Basle), the *Lock* (1876, Paris, London Collection), second rendering of the *Lock* (Geneva), *Floods at Port-Marly* (1876, Louvre), the *Boat* (Louvre), *Spring* (1878), *Saint Mammès* (1884, Geneva), the *Seine at Saint-Cloud* (Lausanne), *Farmyard* (1888). Sisley was very generous with his many drawings, not foreseeing what high prices they were to fetch later. The collector who after Sisley's death acquired the picture *Floods* had to pay 43,000 francs for it. This would have been a fortune to Sisley, yet the painting had stood unsold in his studio for twenty-three years.

Pierre Auguste Renoir (1841—1919) made his official début in the world of French painting at the Salon d'Automne of 1864. Up to then, before joining Bazille, Monet and Sisley, and taking up painting, he had lived as a young, unknown potter at Limoges. The first picture he showed was *Esmeralda*, still romantic in subject; but he soon joined the ranks of Impressionism. In landscape and portraiture (his portraits are numerous) he laid on blobs of paint of various sizes, rubbed them down on the canvas so that the over-all impression was of a palette smeared on to the canvas. We see from his work that he employed Impressionist techniques, which had produced such varied reactions in both critics and public. One cannot but admire the perfection of such paintings as *Rest after the Bath* (Louvre), the *Theatre Box* (1874, London, Courtauld Institute), the *Nymphs* (*c.* 1918, Louvre), the *Luncheon of the Boating Party* (1881, Washington, Phillips Memorial Gallery), and many more. Nobody knew better than Renoir that it is from separate tones that strong light derives its colour (Duranty), ' and that the sun, when reflected by objects, through its own brilliance binds these tones together to a luminous entity in which the spectral colours melt into a homogenous atonality—light.'

One would, however, be mistaken in assuming that Renoir based his technique entirely on theory. His ideas and his feelings, which he knew so well how to express, were on quite a different, one may say, a higher plane. Renoir wrote: ' As the broad masses appear to have failed Catholicism, it seems to be dying, and no substitute for it has been found. God doesn't seem to be wanted any more, yet our imagination cannot get along without him... modern rationalism may be able to satisfy scientists but it will always be incompatible with the concept of art. Rationalism is only a religion for those who would like to build their temple of machines; and this certainly would never accomplish the beauty of Notre-Dame, it could never reach our soul unless it were replaced by reason... in its omnipotent period the Church, often so tyrannical, allowed artists almost unlimited freedom... according to her way of thinking faith was to decide who could fearlessly dare to draw on profane sources... under the influence of Greek culture which shortly afterwards came to Italy and France and was received there with alacrity, the cult of beauty to which Catholicism gave a new aspect appeared once more...'

With regard to the art of his day Renoir (who spent his apprenticeship as an artisan—which he never forgot) was convinced that ' the visual arts were suffering from the fact that manual work no longer required mental effort.' (He was thinking of the consequences which the introduction of machines brought to his century.) ' The desire to ignore these machines explains the quite abnormal number of painters and sculptors who have sprung up and the general mediocrity which has resulted from it... we will try to understand the minor reasons for this increase, the main reason of which is, to my mind, the lack of ideals...'

Though at the beginning of his career Renoir did not escape the petty judgment of conformists, his working life was not too difficult; his portraits pleased the public and he never lacked commissions. Durand-Ruel, a business man, who arranged exhibitions for some artists like Pissarro, Sisley and others who had escaped to England during the war of 1870-71, organised a one-man show of his works. His reputation was consolidated after the Salon of 1879 when he exhibited a painting of the *Charpentier Family*. He travelled extensively. During his stay in Italy he met Richard Wagner in Palermo and painted his portrait. At Aix, he visited Cézanne, with whom he had painted before at L'Estaque. He frequently visited Spain, then Burgundy, and later on he was attracted by the South of France and lived in Provence, where he hoped the climate might cure his arthritis. Eventually, he was forced to paint in a wheel-chair, with brushes tied to his wrist. He lived at Cagnes, near Nice, with his wife who had been his companion and model; she died there in 1915. He survived her for four difficult years and died in 1919, leaving behind him a heritage of beauty.

Let us go back to his portraits: there is a portrait of his father at the City Art Museum of St Louis; a self-portrait in the Taylor Collection at Philadelphia; the portraits of Coco (his son Claude as a child); of *Coco at the Easel*. There are other child portraits, and a portrait of his friend Cézanne. Renoir's particular forte was in portraits of women: *Jeanne Samary, Thérèse Bérard, Gabrielle with a Rose, Woman Writing, Mademoiselle Romaine Lacaux, Woman Reading*, the *Guitar Player, Mademoiselle Sicot*, to mention a few. Some of his nudes are superb, be they of allegorical subjects—the *Source*—or of a more naturalistic kind—as *Reclining Woman*. All of them are distinguished by a harmony of light.

Weigert pointed out clearly that Renoir was particular about his choice of subject (fruit, flowers, vases, genres, crowd scenes). This choice of subject often gave his admirers a pleasant surprise; you need only look at his scenes of the Paris Boulevards and his Algerian landscapes. He painted the elegant *Box at the Paris Opera*, and an ordinary Sunday *plein-air* scene of *Swings*. It is worth noting that in *Ball at Bougival* a couple hop to popular music, whereas in the elegant *Ball in Town* another couple glide along gracefully. In both cases the dynamic of the dance is rendered superbly, as if one could hear the music. The decisive factor in each is mainly the mood, which is created by the techniques of Impressionist painting and by the genius of the artist.

Among the Impressionists we may count some minor artists who were fascinated by the examples of the famous and tried to exhibit a technique of which they were really not fully convinced: the technique which, as Séailles says, 'separates tones to give them greater importance and effect.' To this group belong the following: Henri Martin, who like Renoir painted mainly portraits and thus avoided the financial difficulties which fell to the lot of artists who painted landscapes only; Besnard, who expressed his intense vitality by 'piling on the most vivacious colours yet achieving harmony... so that it seems as if he would outshine the sun' (Reinach); Carrière, who reacted against *plein-air* painting by making his outlines fluid, and 'by plunging his figures into a hazy twilight which underlines their melancholy.' Apart from these painters, the old guard of the movement was still at work. Berthe Morisot, a pupil of Corot's and a sister-in-law of Manet's, was still alive and painting. One of her pictures dating from the year 1881 is *In the Dining Room* (Dale Collection, National Gallery, Washington).

At the same time Lebourg, Lépine, Guillaumin, Monticelli and others who contributed to the spread of genre painting (Ulisse Butin, Lhermitte, Roll, Steinlen) pursued a course which, as Anatole France expressed it, was far removed from the golden shadows of Watteau's parks and their parties where rustling silk whispers of love.

Courbet's and Millet's influences could still be felt. Art preoccupied itself increasingly with the people; the artists depicted factory workers, peasants and street scenes. They adopted a different attitude to these subjects from that of the Dutch painters (Reinach), who merely stressed the picturesque. French art and its social tendencies now showed a deep brotherly sympathy—the same emotion which had moved Millet and Courbet.

We have pointed out that Courbet's and Manet's naturalism led to an idealistic, slightly academic, and symbolic reaction. 'To this reaction the influence of the English pre-Raphaelites contributed. The representatives of this raffiné, aristocratic movement in France were Gustave Moreau and Paul Baudry.' These two painters felt the decorative value of *plein-air* painting, but if we want to look for symbolism, idealism, poetry and philosophy, they are really to be found in the works of Puvis de Chavannes (1824—1898), who painted and decorated the Paris Panthéon. An example of the classical side of his painting is to be found in the picture the *Sacred Grove*. The two Lyons painters Chenavard and Chassériau show a certain kinship to Puvis (they, however, refrain from imitating Giotto).

These are not big names, yet we should like to see an exhibition of the works of these and similar *petits maîtres* which would give a survey of the minor French painters of the period we are dealing with. This epoch so resounds with the names of the famous that one hardly hears the voices of the lesser, yet also deserving, artists.

Edgar Degas (1834—1917) was a friend of Manet's, and also belonged to that gallant group which had accomplished the revolt against rigid academicism. He was a Parisian born and bred; his pictures are of the stage, the race-course and of interiors painted in artificial light. He was a master of mobile perspective, and his artistic interests revolved round such figures as ballerinas, laundresses and milliners; he was inti-

CLAUDE MONET: Spring in Giverny (1882, Private Collection, New York)

Edouard Manet: Portrait of Irma Brunner (1882, Camondo Collection, Louvre, Paris)

EDOUARD MANET: At Argenteuil (1874, Museum of Art, Tournai)

Camille Pissarro: Landscape near Pontoise (1879, Private Collection, New York)

MARY CASSATT: In the Box (pencil drawing)

mately acquainted with their way of living; he had drawn and painted them in every conceivable way—alone and in groups, in the nude and clothed, but always with an eye alert to the piquancy of the situation. In his portraits he catches the sitters in their most intimate moments and gives the painting a mood of tenderness.

Degas also followed *plein-air* painting, but up to a certain point only: then he was drawn to the atmosphere of smoky taverns, which even to this day gives him a reputation of being vulgar. Critics have also called him vulgar because of the many series of women in the nude which he painted (women bathing, women drying themselves after a bath, women combing their hair or having it combed...), mostly in pastels—and because of the very perfection, diligence and care with which he executed them. We, however, maintain that other standards should be applied to work which can only be compared to the paintings of Florentine *ateliers* of the *Quattrocento*.

Louis Gillet, a great connoisseur of French art, points out that Degas was one of the first to ' renew the language of art and enrich its whole vocabulary' by observation of nature and reality. His concern was to catch life unawares, *quasi in flagranti*, and release himself from the pattern of studio painting. This he achieves by feeling for form, movement and plastic values.

Degas loved painting for painting's sake. He admired Ingres and, at the same time, without being untrue to himself, professed great admiration for Delacroix. In Rome he became acquainted with the works of Pisanello, Pollaiuolo, Mantegna, Ghirlandaio and Simone Cronaca, whom Savonarola had commissioned to build the Hall of the Five Hundred, and the Church of San Francesco on the hills of San Miniato.

Degas' beginnings did not foreshadow the personality he was to become. He first did etchings; after a short visit to his brother at New Orleans (1872-3) he painted some classical canvases: *Alexander and Bucephalus*, *Young Spartan Woman*, and the *Disaster of Orléans*, all at the Musée des Capucines in Paris.

At New Orleans he also seemed to have conceived the plan for the picture the *Cotton-Broker's Office at New Orleans*, dated 1873, now at the Museum of Pau.

Though Degas' close connection with Manet had started in 1865, he still exhibited at the Salon of that year a canvas in the conventional style: *Woman with Folded Hands* (Gardner Museum, Boston), a portrait of *Madame Gaujelin*. From then on he never looked back. First he painted the *Orchestra*, then a *Portrait of Madame Camus* followed by one of *Mademoiselle Dichau* and many others.

His ballerinas are well known; looking at these graceful figures in hazy pastels it seems hard to understand that Degas should have been accused of vulgarity. Yet it must be admitted that some of his subjects (for instance *Café Montmartre* and *Absinthe*) are of stark realism. We must not forget, however, that these were the days in which Zola wrote *L'Assommoir*, which evoked such controversy. So Degas' starkness is well in keeping with the times.

A précis of Paul Cézanne's life (1839—1906) as written by André Leclerc has to all appearances the dryness of a legal document; but this is belied by a further acquaintance with Cézanne's life.

Cézanne, born in Aix-en-Provence, was the son of a hatter who later became a rich banker. He was, together with Zola, a pupil at the local college; they made friends, and this friendship was to have a marked influence on Cézanne's life and career.

After taking his Lycée degree, he went to Paris. He refused to go to university and tried for the Academy, where he was rejected for lack of talent! Meanwhile he met Pissarro and Guillaumin. He studied the Old Masters at the Louvre without ever imitating or copying them. (Later he wrote: ' Couture advised his pupils to keep good company, by which he meant to visit the Louvre! Having seen the great masters there one should then quickly leave them alone and commune with oneself and Nature to allow one's own dormant, artistic impulses and sensibilities to awaken.')

Cézanne painted with violence, putting sombre, dense colours on to the canvas with a palette knife. In despair he often destroyed the canvas afterwards. He was also violent in his ways. Nobody, not even Zola, who often had to put up with a lot from his friend, was allowed to interfere with him in any way.

Cézanne was constantly rejected by the Salons. He divided his time in the late 1860's between Aix and Paris, and stayed in L'Estaque in 1870, returning to Paris in 1871. Meanwhile Impressionism had been born, and Cézanne succeeded in being accepted by the group of artists which was to become so famous.

Around 1874 he began to paint in a different way from his colleagues. (This fact must be kept in mind when deciding whether it is justifiable to call Cézanne the grave-digger of Impressionism.) After a few shows, he began to make a reputation for himself and people commissioned him for portraits. The Salon continued to exclude him until 1882, and even then he was not admitted on his merits (he exhibited a portrait), but through the influence of Guillaumin, who sat on the selection committee. A similar incident occurred at the World Exhibition of 1889 when his friend Chocquet was a member of the jury and spoke in his favour.

Cézanne pretended to be immune to these insults and ignored his critics, but in reality he suffered deeply from his isolation. He retired to Aix where, in spite of a considerable fortune left him by his father, he led a precarious and misanthropic life. Now he had lost interest in everything, even in painting. In 1890, however, James Ensor and Theo van Rysselberge (of the Twenty Group) invited him to take part in the Brussels Exhibition; he sent a landscape with a group of bathers, the *Hut at Auvers-sur-Oise*.

In 1895 Ambroise Vollard, the publisher and art-dealer, arranged a show of Cézanne's pictures. It was not difficult to collect them as they lay unsold in the artist's studio. This was the turning-point in Cézanne's career.

In spite of this, Cézanne continued to live in solitude and remained a sombre, unsociable, irritable man who even cold-shouldered admirers who had come to Aix on a pilgrimage to see the great master. It sometimes took him ten years to finish a picture, and he was often so dissatisfied with himself that he tore up in a rage a canvas on which he had worked for months. It is not surprising, therefore, that Zola, with whom Cézanne had broken for good, took him as the model for the main figure, the unsuccessful Lantier, of his novel *L'Oeuvre*.

Cézanne was looked upon by his friends as a man who had failed life and had therefore become a bitter crank. Actually, it was all the same to him. He was not impervious to success, but he wanted to live by his own ideals and to find his own truths. The truth for him was not to be found in the detail and precision of draughtsmanship, but in the reality of contour, surface and colour and their rapport to the object and its surroundings. He never painted what others saw, but only what he saw himself. Before him, most painters thought that a still-life should be composed of original—in themselves beautiful—objects, such as a copper vase, a piece of translucent china, some game, an irridescent fish, luscious fruit or beautiful flowers on an embroidered cloth ... Cézanne was the first to paint humble objects—a bottle, a jug, an apple on a creased tablecloth...

To still-life, until then a rather neglected domain of painting (as says Venturi, whom we are quoting here), Cézanne gave a new impetus and an altogether new significance. He painted inanimate things, such as fruit or a piece of furniture. Painting, it is true, had since time immemorial represented inanimate objects, but usually only as ornaments to enhance the human figure, and very seldom as the only motif of the composition. At the beginning of the seventeenth century, still-life became a new branch of painting, but was looked upon as an imitation of everyday things without any idea behind it, and therefore was not held in any great esteem. With the coming of Cézanne, however, it attained unprecedented importance. The modern painter likes to paint a subject such as an apple because of its very simplicity, which does not distract him from line, form or colour—which are now his means of expressing his own personal feelings. Nothing is likely to render more clearly the artist's disengagement from the things he represents than does still-life.

'... And people now said that whereas the Old Masters painted pictures of the Madonna, the modern ones for lack of inspiration and spiritual interest have taken to painting apples; which is not true—in fact the contrary is true. Imagination has become such a force in modern painting that an apple is now a subject fit to express sublime ideas. The sublime in connection with an apple would seem ridiculous in reality. In art, however, everything is possible as long as the artist looks upon the apple as a means of realising his idea of line, form and colour and refrains from representing that apple in a naturalistic way. The same problem presents itself to the realist who wants to paint a human figure; if he renders all aspects of it in materialistic detail he ceases to be an artist and lowers his standard to that of a mere craftsman—a photographer. This would apply even more to the representation of an apple; as in itself it will always be a less interesting subject than the human form' (Venturi).

The question now arises whether an argument like this is at all pertinent to a work whose main purpose is to serve as a companion text to a comparatively small number of reproductions.

We would rather look with our mind's eye at some of those Impressionist or Neo-Impressionist pictures;

and if we feel a wind blowing or see the blazing sun we know that we are in the presence of Cézanne—the mistral of modern French painting. Provence, his home, to which he always felt nostalgically drawn, has imprinted its character on his still-lifes, his landscapes and his portraits, which are now in all the major galleries of the world. Their luminous colours would in themselves be enough to create form and plastic values. The miracle is that he achieves it all by using almost exclusively reds, yellows and blues. He superimposes a strong blue on a lighter one, paints green leaves on a delicate blue background and achieves contrasts and harmonies with soft tones and most subtle nuances. Light, in his paintings, always shimmers (and that alone would classify him as belonging to the Impressionists), and when he dissolves the contour he respects weight and depth of the object. Cézanne was not influenced by the Venetian painters whom he had studied in Paris; neither could Van Gogh and Gauguin, whom he met in Arles, dissuade him from his chosen path. The Salon d'Automne of 1906 saw him at the peak of his fame. He died following a heart attack at the age of sixty-seven.

He was an industrious worker, both early on in his painting career and later, when, after a change of technique, he opened the way for new movements such as Cubism. Nature must be treated in a geometrical way 'by the cylinder, the sphere, the cone—everything in proper persepctive so that each side of an object is directed towards a central point.' Thus he wrote in a somewhat theorising way about the lines which are parallel with the horizon, giving width, and those running at right angles to the horizon, giving depth.

Among Cézanne's landscapes there are numerous views of *L'Estaque* (Louvre, and various private collections). Among his best-known pictures are *Poplars* (1879-82, Louvre), the *Lake of Annecy* (1896, London, Courtauld Institute), *Mount Sainte-Victoire* (several versions), the well-known still-lifes, and portraits like the ones of *Madame Cézanne*, *Young Man in a Red Waistcoat* (1890-95, Buhrle Collection, Zürich), *Ambroise Vollard* (1899), and some self-portraits. He painted a famous series of *Card Players*, and one of *Bathers*.

VII

Georges Seurat (1859—1891) had been the real driving force of Impressionism, according to Verhaeren, and Van Gogh had called him the head of the movement; Seurat 'searched the unknown and found it more than did others.' Reducing this exaggeration to a tolerable measure, as does Cogniat, it follows that this painter concentrated on the study of light and colour and integrated and disciplined his obervations to formulate a law and system which should co-ordinate the intentions of the Impressionists with the scientific discoveries of the time. At first sight it would appear as if intellect had supremacy over his art, that his ideas did not come as quickly as his theoretical calculations: in short, that he had more confidence in a well prepared palette than in spontaneous artistic instinct, that his aim was not the work of art proper but a striving for a purely technical co-ordination between the luminosity of colour and the composition of form. Yet we have to admire the, deep feeling and expressiveness of his main works. (How many would he not have created had he not died at the age of thirty-one!) Some of his paintings are: *La Grande Jatte* (1885, Art Institute, Chicago), *Le Chahut* (1889-90, Albright Art Gallery, Buffalo), the *Harbour of Honfleur* (1886, Barnes Foundation, Merion, Pennsylvania), *Le Cirque* (1891, Louvre), *Une Baignade, Asnières* (1883-84, Tate Gallery, London), *Nurse with Child*, the *Stonebreaker*, *Peasant*. It seems difficult to reconcile ourselves to the idea that the starting point for paintings as original as these should have been based on purely scientific research in connection with the stearine candle.

Before Seurat embarked on the hazardous venture of Divisionism (or Pointillism) he consulted Michel Chevreul, who held the patent for this candle. Chevreul was a chemist, professor of applied colour chemistry and head of the laboratory of the famous Gobelin tapestry works. Chevreul's theories (and practical experience) helped Seurat in creating *La Grande Jatte*, the first and last picture to be shown at an exhibition (the eighth Impressionist exhibition, of 1886) that had been painted 'only in pure divided, harmonising colours which blend optically according to a preconceived process; it was to become the basis of Neo-Impressionism.' Paul Signac and Henri Cross, two faithful followers of Divisionism, testified to that; later Pissarro, Van Gogh, Matisse and Braque were to give it up, in spite of having achieved success with it.

PIERRE AUGUSTE RENOIR: Alfred Sisley and his Wife (1868, Wallraf-Richartz Museum, Cologne)

PIERRE AUGUSTE RENOIR: Lady with a Veil (Louvre, Paris)

74

CLAUDE MONET: Hôtel de la Plage (Private Collection, Paris)

PIERRE AUGUSTE RENOIR: Portrait of a Young Girl (lithograph)

← BERTHE MORISOT: In the Dining Room (1881, Chester Dale Collection, National Gallery of Art, Washington)

With Seurat the terms Neo-Impressionism and Post-Impressionism were coined. They cover, generally speaking, the movements based on the discoveries of the Impressionists and developed in French painting after 1880, 'as a reaction, one may say, to their naturalism and the confidence with which they gave themselves up to their feeling of reality.' Seurat and Signac, the discoverers of Divisionism, put, with intellectual, doctrinal strictness, the scientific findings in the field of light and colour to the service of art. The balance between Nature and self-expression which the Impressionists had realised broke down with the Post-Impressionists who followed them and repeated and modified their experiments. This destroyed the value of the technique of form and colour which the Impressionists had so scrupulously attuned to their subject-objective Nature. Thus matters could reach a point when it was possible for Van Gogh to give his colours such strength and glow that they violated nature.

Vincent Van Gogh (1853—1890), Dutch by birth, was in his art neither Dutch nor French, nor in fact of any country. He created out of himself, his restlessness, about which one hears so much and knows so little. Once on the subject of Van Gogh one cannot be brief, nevertheless we can only give a few sketchy biographical notes here. The rest must be done by the critics who, as yet, have not even come to a conclusive judgment on his work.

From the list of biographies of artists in the appendix of one of Cogniat's books we get a useful hint: never again to write about Van Gogh's private life; his spiritual and financial miseries have been thrashed out too often. It seems sad that so many people show more interest in the tragic events of his life than in the glory of his work. It is in any case difficult to separate the one from the other because we find in the brilliant pictures of Van Gogh the signs of mental disturbance. The emotional power of his work is determined by the intensity of his feelings, and therefore onedoes not err in finding the reflection of the one in the other.

At the time when Van Gogh was full of infinite pity for mankind in general and for the miners of the Borinage in particular, he wanted to become a Protestant minister (he came from a Protestant family), and to be able to live with the miners and help them. At this time his art became harsh, his drawing hard and his colours sombre. Only when various discouraging experiences led him to believe that he was excluded from mankind, did he devote his whole life to painting. He then expressed his high ideals in glorious colour and a passionate technique in which every brush-stroke seemed to be laid on with violence. The more love was denied Van Gogh, the more the strength of his work increased. His disappointments began early, perhaps at the time when, as an unmanageable boy, he did not take part in the games of his playmates, and even avoided the company of his brothers. In London, where as a youth he was sent to learn 'how to cope with life,' he proposed to a girl who rejected him; this caused him great suffering. He was constantly at odds with his family who didn't understand his character—so different from the ordinary; quarrels alternated with reconciliations. A niece of his refused his offer of marriage. Other disappointments, about which one does not know enough, followed. Then he had the noble but impractical idea of reforming a prostitute. Always, his willingness to sacrifice himself met with a general lack of understanding (Venturi says of him that he was a missionary who continually preached even by means of his painting), which condemned him to loneliness and eventually paved the way to tragedy. Here his friendship with Gauguin comes to mind, the ending of which nearly meant the end of life to one of them (1888). It was then that Van Gogh mutilated his left ear with a razorblade as a self-punishment for having threatened his friend. (That is only one of the various versions of this story). Two years later Van Gogh ended the tragic vacillation between violent periods of hallucination and uncanny intervals of calmness with a revolver.

Van Gogh's art was vehement. From it, Expressionism, which was an attempt to liberate man from despair, was to develop. In Van Gogh's picture an intense, golden yellow prevails, which spreads over the whole canvas; he also used a brilliant red. Let us listen to the artist himself and to what he has to say about the variety of tones at his disposal which enabled him to attain such moods as the following: 'In my picture the *Night Café* I tried to show that a tavern is a place where one can ruin oneself, run mad or commit a crime. This I tried to express by using delicate pink, blood red and dark burgundy in contrast, by subtle green *à la Louis Quinze*, and by green *à la Veronese* which I set against a yellowish-green and a hard bluish-green. All this expresses the atmosphere of a tangled milieu full of sick suffering.'

His brush-stroke is incisive, ragged and contorted, alive, like a fiery tongue. From his former association with Gauguin, he retained an overwhelming striving for pure accentuated colours put into contrast and for the absence of shade. Among the best known of his pictures are: the *Sunflowers*, the *Gladioli*, the *Self-portraits*, the views of the *Alyscamps*, the Provence landscapes, *Crows over a Cornfield*, the *Starry Night* and finally the *Town Hall at Auvers*, which is easily the gayest and most festive of his pictures, as befits the subject. It shows flags and Chinese lanterns (but no human sitter) on the national holiday in a little village. This canvas bears in fact the date July 14th, 1890—a fortnight before his suicide.

Paul Gauguin (1848—1903) was to form with Van Gogh that turbulent twin constellation which disturbed the horizons of the outgoing nineteenth century. His exoticism may have been due to the Peruvian blood of his mother, and is apt to make one forget that he was a true Parisian. He spent the first four years of his life in Lima; only after the death of his father, a political exile, did he return to France with his mother. At the early age of nine he showed a vagrant tendency; he tied a bundle filled with sand on a stick and with this for luggage tried to break out in search of adventure. He was caught and placed in the College of Orléans, from which he took French leave at the age of sixteen to become a sailor in the Merchant Navy. After six years he gave up his seafaring life, although he had by then become a helmsman in the Navy proper. A young Danish girl, Mette Gad, brought him to his senses. She became his wife, and for her sake he became a stockbroker. Gauguin's only free time was on Sundays, when, as a modest, solitary, week-end painter, he tried his luck at the easel. Then he met Pissarro and came to know the Impressionists. As long as he could he tried to resist the temptation of a free life dedicated to art, but in 1883 he gave up his job. About this time his wife, whose financial position had become desperate, returned with their five children to her family in Denmark. Gauguin followed her in despair; too proud to depend on anybody he took employment with a business man in the provinces, where, one day, furious at wasting his time with work he hated, he attacked a client and was dismissed. He returned to Paris, taking one of his sons with him. The other children stayed with their mother in Copenhagen where she was trying to eke out a living translating Zola into Danish. Even later, when he tried to make a better life for his son and to give his wife some financial help, there was no reconciliation, so he decided to leave the humiliations of employment for a life on a solitary beach away from human company.

He went to Pont-Aven, in Brittany. There the peasants were as simple and clumsy as he was to portray them; they allowed him to decorate the walls of their little chapels with religious figures—primitive and stiff. The curate of Pont-Aven, however, was scandalised by his *Jacob and the Angel*, which he rejected.

From now on, Gauguin ascribed to colour a new, sensual, symbolic and literary significance unrelated to the real image of objects, 'beyond the borderline of the visible'.

The boy who, with a bundle over his shoulder, had tried to go in search of adventure, thirty years later tried to do the same. Now he did not take a bundle of sand with him, but he did not take much else. In the company of the painter Laval, he left France in 1887. They stopped at Panama; the canal was just being built, and Gauguin put in a twelve hour working day with a pickaxe to make some money. From there they went to Martinique where they both nearly died of fever and dysentery. Gauguin returned to Paris a defeated man. The public did not appreciate the few pictures he had done on the other side of the ocean. He now began to make plaster casts to earn a living, but returned as soon as possible to Pont-Aven, where his ideas began to shape themselves into a system and where he did a *Portrait of Maria Henry*, his landlady.

The turbulent interlude in Arles, where he had gone to meet Van Gogh, is well known. In spite of many quarrels, they had considerable influence on each other. Van Gogh taught Gauguin the technique of the Japanese, their pictorial language, as it were. Gauguin convinced Van Gogh that colour and line carry a message which should be suggested rather than outspoken.

His penultimate voyage (1891) was to Tahiti; he found Papeete uncivilised so he went on to Mataica and lived there with a 'gentle, quiet' Tahitian girl of thirteen. He went on painting and hoped the French Ministry of Public Instruction and Fine Arts, which had made vague promises, would buy his pictures. In 1893 he returned to Paris, an ill, unhappy man. To his disappointment, his friend at the Ministry had left, and the new man in charge would not honour any of the former agreements, moreover he refused to buy *Manao Tupapau*, the picture in which Gauguin expressed the mystical fear that lives in the heart of the natives (Leclerc).

He tried to settle in Paris; disaster followed disaster. He took a Javanese woman on a trip to Brittany; a quarrel about her broke out between Gauguin and some sailors, who nearly killed him. While he was ill in hospital, the woman stole his belongings and even emptied his studio of its furniture. At the same time his daughter Aline, who had been the only member of his family who loved, admired and at times supported him, died. The fight with the sailors had left him with a slight but permanent infirmity. From now on he could not stand France; the civilisation of the white man disgusted him.

He returned to Tahiti only to find it changed too. He took employment in Papeete, and tried to find his old hut which had now tumbled down and was infested with pests. His whole being protested against these misfortunes; a grief-stricken man, he cried out in anguish. This anguish manifests itself in the blue and green triptych with its orange figures to which he gave the title: *Whence do we come—What are we—Where are we going?* (1897, Museum of Fine Arts, Boston).

The authorities at Papeete disliked him for his eccentricities. He had to leave and chose Hiva-Oa in the Marquesas Islands to settle. He built a studio and furnished and decorated it. He called it the *Maison du Jouir* and lived happily there. In 1902 a painting, the *Call*, reflects his serene, almost bucolic mood.

He soon made friends with the natives, whose relations with the white authorities of the island were strained. He was now accused of inciting them to rebellion. He decided to go to Tahiti to contest the verdict—but this was never to happen. Gauguin died in his lonely hut on May 8th, 1903.

Among his most important works are: the *Seine at the Pont d'Iéna* (1875, Louvre), the *Yellow Christ* (1889, Albright Art Gallery, Buffalo), *Landscape: Le Pouldu* (1890), his portraits of Breton women, and other portraits and self-portraits, all painted before 1890. Now follows Gauguin's exotic period: *Women of Tahiti*, the *Idol*, *Vahine No Te Tiare* (the Woman with a Flower), *When Shall we be Married?*, the *Moon and the Earth*, *Te Rerioa* (the Dream), the *White Horse* and *Riders on the Beach*.

Gauguin was also Post-Impressionist in his sculpture. There exists a self-portrait in this medium which he himself called the *Savage*.

Henri de Toulouse-Lautrec (1864—1901) was of noble birth. He spent his early years and young manhood at his parental homes, at Albi and Malromé in the South of France. As a boy he fell and broke a leg; a year later, still suffering from the consequences of the first fall, he had another, which this time was to cripple him for life. It also stunted his growth. He completed his education, which he had begun at the Lycée Condorcet in Paris, at home.

Infirmity excluded him from sport and social life. Painting was the only means of keeping up his spirits, and once he had started it, he was never to give it up. He loved to paint horses: the *Amazon and her Groom*, the *Dogcart*, the *Gunner Leading Two Horses* and the *Four-In-Hand*—a portrait of his father driving, which has the immediacy of a snapshot. These pictures, of which the first three are at the Albi Museum and the fourth at the Petit Palais in Paris, were all painted between 1879 and 1881. They are strikingly Impressionistic in movement.

Toulouse-Lautrec went to Paris to study painting. His first teacher was Princeteau, a friend of the family. Later on he became a pupil of Bonnat and Cormon, neither of whom could do much for him. Meanwhile the lights, the noise and the café life of Montmartre began to fascinate him. Women could not play a part in his life, yet he wanted to be surrounded by them, and his paintings are full of the shady, frivolous figures of the girls of the Moulin de la Galette, the Moulin Rouge, and the Divan Japonais. He loved the circus, and his circus scenes, mainly of horses, are superb. His output was vast. Besides drawings and lithographs there were many portraits—of *Van Gogh* in his most serene and humane mood, of *Oscar Wilde*, with whom he remained friends in spite of Wilde's later notoriety. Some others, almost in a caricaturist vein (*May Belfort, Maxime de Thomas*, the *Englishman at the Moulin Rouge, Monsieur Boileau at the Café*), are yet masterpieces of psychological insight. But however sarcastic, depraved and miserable Toulouse-Lautrec may appear to us, the portrait of his mother, the *Comtesse de Toulouse-Lautrec*, shows tenderness and feeling.

The complete breakdown he suffered may have been accelerated by his dissolute way of life, but probably more by his untiring, hectic work. He was a contributor to *Rire*, the *Mercure de France* and the *Revue Blanche*. He also illustrated luxury editions of books.

PIERRE AUGUSTE RENOIR: Girl with a Watering-can (detail)
(Chester Dale Collection, National Gallery of Art, Washington)

PIERRE AUGUSTE RENOIR: Young Girl (1883, Metropolitan Museum of Art, New York)

PAUL CÉZANNE: Portrait of Madame Cézanne (1887, Louis E. Stern Collection, New York)

PIERRE AUGUSTE RENOIR: The Luncheon of the Boating Party (1881, Phillips Memorial Gallery, Washington)

84

EDGAR DEGAS: After the Bath (drawing)

EDGAR DEGAS: Dancer (water-colour)

PIERRE AUGUSTE RENOIR: Women Bathing (water-colour and crayon)

He had no great theories about painting and consequently no coherent technique. The incisive immediacy of his paintings, the lack of black and neutral tones classify him as an Impressionist; however, he was not preoccupied with colour contrasts, which had been Manet's personal invention.

Henri Rousseau (1844—1910) does not seem to have been able to shake off the somewhat derogatory nickname of *le Douanier*. Rousseau, who was employed as a customs officer and painted on Sundays only, succeeded nevertheless in attracting the attention of serious artists, of the critics and the public. Vlaminck and Picasso appreciated him; amateurs thought there was life in his pictures which express a strong artistic personality.

It would seem doubtful, however, to maintain, as some have, that he continued the artistic tradition of Nicolas Poussin. The comparaison here may be that Rousseau, like Poussin, saw the art of painting as the imitation of all things visible which could be represented in line and colour on canvas.

Controversy round Rousseau continues, though it is more temperate today. Those who call Rousseau 'the father of all primitives' put less stress on his naive qualities than on his awareness of the exigencies of artistic vision. He was instinctively and unconsciously opposed to the synthetic, fluid forms of Impressionism and so his own forms were analytical and of firm contours, as illustrated by the *Snake Charmer*, *War*, the *Poet and his Muse* and many exotic landscapes.

Odilon Redon (1840—1916) came from Bordeaux. He was by no means a primitive painter but on the contrary a precious, rare colourist who in both oils and pastels created a fantastic world of 'intoxicating mysterious flowers, strange figures of women, archangels winged like butterflies, magic oriental visions of praying Buddhas surrounded by flowers.'

All his pictures show (to use his own words) that he wanted to make each one of them 'a little door opening on to mystery.' (See *A Soi-Même*, *Journal et Notes*, and Grohmann's Bibliography in Thiene-Becker's

Pierre Auguste Renoir: Study (red chalk drawing)

Künstler Lexikon, Leipzig, 1934.) His technique is pleasing; he tries to put the world of plants and animals on a level with humanity. 'In art,' he says, 'nothing is done by will alone. Everything is done by docile submission to what comes from the unconscious.' But to him this submission is really conscious, and he can therefore give depth to the dreams of the unconscious. Redon does not belong to any school or group. In spite of the meticulous, brilliant technique shown in his paintings, lithographs and engravings, the dominant power in his work remains imagination and poetic sensibility.

We now come to the more recent painters. Chronological order seems to be difficult: Modigliani, for instance, who died in 1920, undoubtedly seems 'more modern' than do Vuillard, Denis and even Bonnard, who died in 1940, 1943 and 1947 respectively.

Edouard Vuillard (1868—1940) was known as a member of the Nabis, a group of symbolic and decorative painters, but his own personality soon became evident in the intimate character of his pictures, inspired by Verlaine whom he passionately admired. His portraits are mostly set in interiors of a velvety atmosphere, which he achieved by a painstaking Pointillistic technique, as in the portraits of *Théodore Duret* and *Siga Kapfere*. They are of rich, harmonious, blended colours and are of a decorative style. The paintings at the Théâtre des Champs Elysées and the four big panels (after Japanese motifs) at the Petit Palais, are also good examples of this style.

Maurice Denis (1870—1943) also belongs to decorative art. He painted (at the time that Vuillard worked there) the ceiling of the Théâtre des Champs Elysées with four magnificent scenes representing the Muses. Gillet called these 'the most brilliant example of French decorative art since Puvis de Chavannes.'

Denis, like his colleagues Sérusier and Roussel (all pupils of Lefèbvre), was opposed to Naturalism; he was drawn to Gauguin's Primitivism and Cézanne's light-effects. He frequently went to Italy which influenced his choice of colour and his balanced line-drawing. Denis first impressed the public in 1891 with *Easter Secret*, then, in 1892, with the *Nativity*. In both these pictures he shows most delicate sensibility. His works of 1895, such as the *Annunciation*, confirm his artistic personality. From then onwards, until 1903, he showed regularly at the Salon des Indépendants. He was a co-founder of the Salon d'Automne, and after 1925 he also exhibited at the Salon des Tuileries. Denis is looked upon as one of the most important representatives of French painting but at the same time his manner is to be considered as Italianised. He wrote a book on Italy (*Notes sur l'Italie*). He published theses in which he expounded his aesthetic theories (*Théories, Nouvelles Théories*, etc.).

Pierre Bonnard (1867—1947) formed, together with Denis, Sérusier, Roussel and others of the Académie Julian a group which was united by their communal enthusiasm for Gauguin 'and the message his art conveyed to them.'

Many years later, however, Cogniat asked Bonnard whether his special love of Gauguin had been a reaction to Impressionism, to which he answered: 'No, not at all... I remember that I didn't know anything of Impressionism at that time; Gauguin's work inspired me for its own sake and not because it was opposed to any other work. We were also enthusiastic when a little later we discovered Impressionism... Gauguin, you know, is almost a conventional classicist; it was Impressionism that gave us freedom.'

Bonnard had no revolutionary ideas about painting; the innovations which he introduced were neither premeditated nor did they intentionally try to evoke polemics. He was not a fighter; he either made use of the experiences of other painters if they conformed to his own ideas, or rejected them if they were against his own sensibilities and would have meant imitation. 'His work is reminiscent of the Impressionists because he has the same divided brush-stroke, the superimposition of colours and the shimmering light. The layout of his pictures and their soft, muted harmonies also have an element of Japanese art. They remind us of Degas and Toulouse-Lautrec because of a certain *angle de vue* and the importance Bonnard gives to the first plane.' It seems hard to believe that the independent technique of an artist like Bonnard, who lived through the violent currents which shook the world of art at the time (between 1920 and 1940) and to which he seems to have been impervious, should not have become static.

He used a brilliant palette to achieve the luminosity of his pictures in which the splendour of *plein-soleil* was contrasted with intensive counter-light effects. 'He created still-lifes sparkling with vivid reds and greens and treated the canvas for what it is: a plane ignoring perspective and its vanishing lines.' Bonnard's art is bold and temperate, modest and original; he is looked upon as the last representative of a bygone epoch and its style. The work he left behind consisted of many portraits, such as: *Boy, Lady with Dog, Lady in a Red Dress, Lady at Breakfast,* the *Portrait of Claude Terrasse* and *Portrait of Edouard Vuillard.* He also painted many female nudes, interiors, and views of Paris (published by Vuillard under the title *Quelques Aspects de la Vie de Paris*). He was also an excellent lithographer, both in black-and-white and in colour, and as such worked for the *Revue Blanche* and *L'Escaramouche.* His glowing scale of colours shows in the *Still-Life* of the Petridés Collection (Paris), in the *White Cupboard* (1933), and also in the *Yellow Shawl,* dated the same year.

Some tried to find in Bonnard's work relations to Ribera; these, however, could only be of a cultural nature (both of them having had an academic education). One might just as well find a remote relationship between Ricard and Titian, Regnault and Goya, Carolus-Duran and Velasquez, Henner and Correggio, Roybet and Frans Hals, Lely and Van Dyck, Bail and Vermeer, Bastien-Lepage and Holbein the Younger, Benjamin Constant and the Venetian Masters. This enumeration is Reinach's. Offshoots of the movements mentioned in this chapter are still alive in the middle of the twentieth century.

VIII

This condensed survey has so far been dealing with French artists only and has neglected quite remarkable works of painters in other parts of Europe. Now to discuss some German artists, the first among them Adolf von Menzel (1815—1905): he was no longer a young man when he began to adopt Impressionist ways. He painted various scenes of contemporary life, such as concerts, markets, factories (among them the famous *Foundry*). He is, however, best known as the chronicler of the Hohenzollern family; in his historic paintings he glorified the achievements of Frederick the Great and other members of the reigning house (the *Coronation of Wilhelm I*). A weakness in his right hand forced him to paint left-handed. He was also a lithographer (*History of Frederick the Great*), and he did woodcuts (*Illustrations to Chamisso's Peter Schlemihl*). Some of his most important works were: *Consultation with the Lawyer* (1837), *Banquet at Sans-Souci* (1850), *Flute Concert of Frederick the Great at Sans-Souci* (1852), *Frederick the Great on a Journey* (1854), and some landscapes which are distinguished by meticulous rendering and logical composition. Menzel's main passion, however, was for military uniforms, gorgeous apparel, burlesque scenes and episodes from the life of the people—in short everything connected with vivid movement.

Arnold Böcklin (1827—1901) was born in Basle, and later became a professor in Weimar. He was a favourite of Ludwig II of Bavaria, for whom he painted a number of pictures, among them *Pan in the Reeds* (1859). Böcklin was a painter in the traditional manner, which accounts for his choice of subjects: mythological scenes (*Triton and Nereid*); his technique, however, was anything but conventional; his symbolism (*Family of Tritons, Family of Sea Creatures*) Mia Cinotti thinks of as having a less formalistic technique than that of Hans von Marées (whom, we may remember, she called a forerunner of Gauguin).

We have already devoted a section to Feuerbach. Böcklin and von Marées supported the realism of the Munich School, whose leaders were Hans Thoma (1839—1924) and Wilhelm Leibl (1844—1900). In one of Leibl's portraits, *Mayor Klein*, which is mellow in its colour, he used an enamel varnish that gave a vitreous firmness to the surface. A *Portrait of the Countess Treuberg* was known as 'one of the most beautiful portraits' of the decade between 1870 and 1880. After 1890, Leibl did *Portrait of Geheimrat Seeger, Man Reading a Newspaper, Portrait of his Niece* and *Portrait of Lina Kirchhoffer.*

Leibl was first a pupil of Strähuber and Anschütz, later of Ramberg and Piloty. In 1869, he met Courbet in Munich and became a follower of his. After this meeting the social tendency of Leibl's paintings and engravings showed his admiration for Courbet.

The Viennese Moritz von Schwind, a painter of mediaeval, archaistic stories and legends is today as good as forgotten. The Nazarene School seems to be better remembered. Some German painters who worked in Rome, Overbeck, Führig and Schnorr, like the pre-Raphaelites round Rossetti, decided on a return to the Quattrocento. They had, however, little success. In Vienna, Hans Makart tried to reintroduce Neo-Venetianism by attempting to revive the Venetian masters' colours. Franz von Lenbach painted portraits of *Wilhelm I* and *Wilhelm II*, works which one may say were more impressive than subtle. Uhde, a mystic, was a direct descendant of French realism, as was Max Liebermann whose work was concerned with social problems. Max Linder, painter, sculptor and engraver, was so highly original an artist that his nonconformity seems justified. He was the outstanding figure of a national movement which, however, before 1914 had no opportunity of proving its originality and independence.

Now to Belgium and Holland, where at the beginning of the nineteenth century artists were also carried along with the tide of Neoclassicism. (Gallait, Leys, and Wauters stemmed from David, and so they partly reflected French Neoclassicism and partly continued the old tradition of the Flemish and Dutch masters of the seventeenth century.) The main representative painters were Pienemann and Scheffer (both Neoclassical) and Spoel, Cool and Schmidt, all historical painters with a tendency towards Romanticism. By and by the Naturalists, among them Schelfout and Bilders, came to the fore; their choice of subject became more and more sentimental. Jozef Israels founded the School of The Hague (which reminds one of the Barbizon School). Bosboom, a forerunner of that school which comprised landscape painters of whom Holland can be proud, had anticipated their ideas. Most of them were talented, it is true, but were amazingly poor in their choice of colours (like Mesdag, Mauve, the three Jacob brothers, Matthias and Wilhelm Maris, of whom one is more sentimental than the other). They were related to other competent landscape painters such as Apol, de Bock and Witsen. Beside these, there were portrait painters like Veht and the followers of Millet who represented scenes of the lives of peasants and fishermen. (Sadée was their leader.) Later on, at the time when Van Gogh moved to France, Breitner and Verster were famous Dutch colourists.

The most famous Dutch painter of recent years has been Piet Mondrian (1872—1944) who formed the de Stijl group and founded Neo-Plasticism.

Tiepolo's decorative art and Canaletto's city scenes had brought fame to Italian art in the eighteenth century but now it began to free itself from these influences. Artistic development was here in step with historic events. Under the reign of the Hapsburgs there was a Neoclassical movement of the strictest kind with Andrea Appiani (1754—1817) as its leader. Romanticism with Francesco Hayez (1791—1882) as its representative began with the national revolution and spread with increasing political independence. When Impressionist art came to Italy, the political climate was anything but calm. One could feel the first symptoms of a social development which was soon to have its effect on the customs, the laws and the economic position of the reborn Italian nation.

Impressionism in Italy had an immediate forerunner in the Tuscan School of the *Macchiaioli*. Its followers were neither academic nor outspokenly anti-academic; only (between 1850 and 1870) with the unification of Italy drawing nearer, did artists become aware of the freedom in their own sphere. So it happened that the Café Michelangelo in Florence (so like the Café Guerbois in Paris, and yet so different) became the headquarters ot the generation of artists round Telemaco Signorini (1835—1901) and, at the same time, the meeting-place of the Italian patriots. It was in that café that the enthusiastic student volunteers drained their last glass before they left to meet the Austrians at Curtatone and Montanara.

Though Macchiaiolism was born in Florence it is taking a geographical liberty to call it Tuscan, as we find among its most competent representatives men who were from other parts of the country. Thus Fattori came from Leghorn, Borrani from Pisa, Giovanni Costa from Rome, Silvestro Lega from the Romagna, Cabianca and Abbati (whose father was Neapolitan) from Venice, Vito d'Ancona from Pesaro, Giovanni Boldini from Ferrara. De Nittis and some others belonging to the group were born in different parts of the peninsula; only Banti, Sernese and Cecioni were Florentine born and bred. The group got its name from its technique and style of painting: these painters put dots of colour (the Italian for which is macchia) on to the canvas and blended them according to their tonal values of light and dark; but the programme of these innovators, especially of Signorini and Fattori, aimed higher than that. They wished to inaugurate a 'purely Italian' style of painting; they wanted Italian painting to speak, as it were its own native tongue.

CAMILLE PISSARRO: Peasant Woman Kneeling (pencil drawing)

PIERRE AUGUSTE RENOIR: Study (1890, Private Collection, Paris) →

PIERRE AUGUSTE RENOIR: Landscape (1890, Renaud Collection, Paris)

EDOUARD MANET: Chez Père Lathuille (1879, Museum of Art, Tournai)

MARY CASSATT: After the Bath (Cleveland Museum of Art, U.S.A.)

This does not mean that Hayez in his portraits, or Gigante who had widened the scope of landscape painting, or the Indunos with their special gift for observation and expression (not to mention many others) had expressed themselves in a foreign tongue—they had merely used different dialects.

Somarè had this to say: 'In England, France and Germany there had not, in spite of diverse tendencies, been any diverse regional schools; not so, however, in Italy where every cultural centre from Venice to Milan, from Florence to Naples, had had its own artists; and this was to remain so, the only change being that for the first time these various schools showed a simultaneous development which converged in communal results and united them into one homogeneous circle. This diversity of schools,' continues Somarè, 'may have prevented Italian painting from developing one dominant style as had Impressionism in France; but it may as a compensation have preserved to Italian painting a variety of techniques, an originality all its own, a frankness in the choice of subject, and copious ways of expression, which gave it a singular richness. This very richness saved it from the danger which always goes with excessive centralisation: that of ending up in mannerism and aestheticism...'

Considering the simultaneity and conformity of these various regional schools one could deal with them *en bloc* without making the mistake of singling out one 'of the totality' of art in Italy at the time.

Let us now briefly mention the new Lombard School, whose most eminent representatives were, besides the Indunos, Piccio (Giovanni Carnovali, 1806—1873), Tranquillo Cremona (1837—1878), Mosè Bianchi (1840—1904), Pelizza da Volpedo (1868—1907), Filippo Carcano (1840—1914), Gaetano Previati (1852—1920), Daniele Ranzoni and Gignous.

The Impressionism of these last-mentioned painters became more and more exaggerated and approached Divisionism. Divisionism is the logical consequence of Impressionist theory (Cochin), which was, in short, the division of light rays. But Divisionism—to repeat the well-known definition—is the endeavour 'not to render light by mixing colours on the palette and then putting them on to the canvas, keeping their relative tonalities, but by dividing the colours on the palette and putting them on to the canvas one separate from the other so as to achieve the relation of complementary colours.' Divisionism, therefore, means what Cézanne expressed by *réalisation* of the motif.

Giovanni Segantini (1858—1899), 'also a Divisionist,' says Ugo Ojetti, 'was only a painter because he was a poet. He loved the mountains which to him conveyed the message that beauty was not of a sensual but of a spiritual nature. With passionate fanaticism he went in search of more and more light; light to him was the visible manifestation of the spirit which reigns harmoniously over all aspects of life. The same sun shines on all the perennial, fluctuating, floating forces of life.'

This shy, lonely painter of solitude, this herald of the alpine world became popular because his art was universal. The main stages of his artistic career are marked by: *Woman Selling Fish* (1879, Rondo Collection, Novara), the *Vessel* Milan *by the Bridge of San Marco* (1880, Marzotto Collection, Valdagno), *At the Bar* (1886, Gallery of Modern Art, Rome), *Ploughing in the Engadine* (1890, New Pinakothek, Munich), *The Two Mothers* (1890, Gallery of Modern Art, Rome), *The Angel of Life* (1894, Gallery of Modern Art, Milan), and the first three panels of the unfinished triptych *Spring* (1897), *Life and Nature* (1897-99, Segantini Museum, St Moritz). Segantini died in the mountains on a glacier of the Schafberg where he placed his easel facing the marvellous mountain range between the Bernina and Julier passes which he intended to paint.

The contribution of Venice and the Veneto to Italian art of the nineteenth century consisted of the works of Favretto, Luigi Nono, Pietro Fragiacomo and the Ciardis. Piedmontese painting passed from the Romantic to the Naturalist Massimo d'Azeglio and then to the Romantic Realist Antonio Fontanesi (1818—1882), a Piedmontese by adoption and to the Impressionist Delleani.

In Southern Italy the Posillipo School was leading; but in the first half of the nineteenth century the influence of Flemish Naturalism and the late reverberations of the *Seicento*, in which Neapolitan influence had been prevalent, were still noticeable. Then, however, De Nittis took the initiative and, as Somarè puts it, 'with his subjectivated objectivity' bridged the gap between reality itself and the feeling for reality. At the same time Filippo Palizzi went on with his physical experiments and Domenico Morelli propounded his idealistic principles. The school of Resina, headed by Federico Rossano and Marco de Gregorio, took the lead

PAUL CÉZANNE: Cézanne's House (water-colour)

in this programme. Succeeding that school and independent of it, Naples and the South were represented by Michele Cammarano, Eduardo Dalbono and F. P. Michetti: this brings us to the end of the nineteenth century. Here Antonio Mancini (1852—1930) should be mentioned as playing an important part; he belongs partly to our century but was remarkably impervious to the new movements in art.

His beliefs, which were of the nineteenth century, allowed him to remain untouched by the art of our time. He was not the only one. The Lombard Emilio Gola, the Tuscan Armando Spadini, Mario Puccini and some others continued quietly painting in a way which was in keeping with their training, their careers up to then, and their age. They painted as they had always done—without impairing the results achieved, and it could not be said that these results were bad.

Amedeo Modigliani (1884—1920) was an Italian who lived and worked in Paris. His output and the intensity of his work was one long challenge to the current artistic movement: the imitation of reality. After living in Florence, Rome and Venice he settled in Paris in 1906. Before that he had been a pupil of Micheli at Leghorn. Micheli himself had been a pupil of Fattori, a bold, competent colourist and interpreter of sea-scapes, who had gone over from Macchiaiolism to Impressionism. In Paris Modigliani led a truly bohemian life; he tried his hand at sculpture, creating heads in the manner of African sculpture, which had lately made its appearance in Europe. These heads, done in stone, were squashed, elongated and stylised. Modigliani's 'happy barbarians' could, in every way but the financial, have been called successful. He adopted the same style in painting. He never painted from the live model. His canvases *Beggar from Leghorn* and the *Cellist* were on show at the Salon des Indépendants of 1910. Later on his paintings were mainly of women: reclining

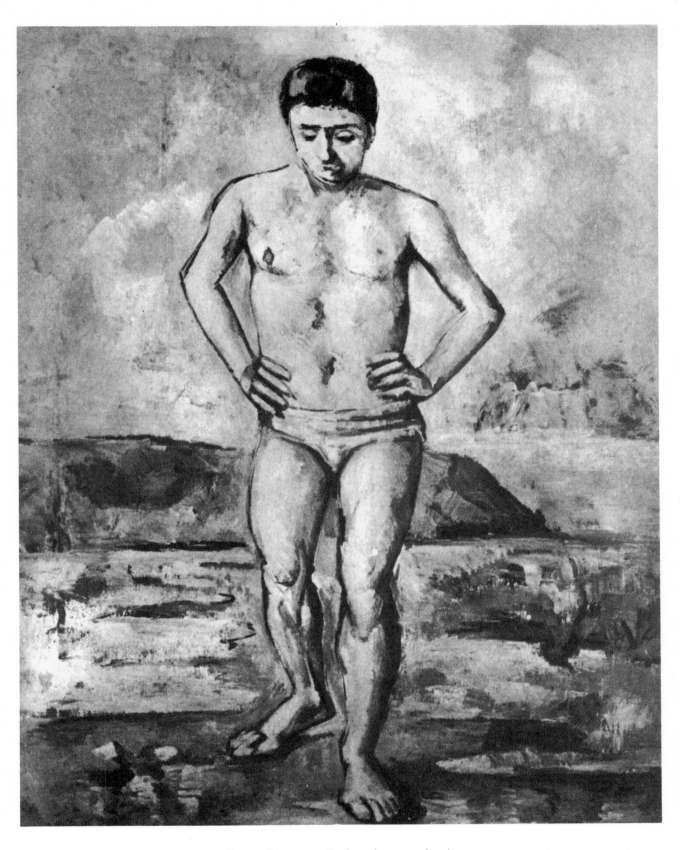

PAUL CÉZANNE: Bather (water-colour)

PAUL CÉZANNE: Self-portrait (drawing)

EDGAR DEGAS: Portrait of Mlle Dobigny (Kunsthalle, Hamburg)

PIERRE AUGUSTE RENOIR: Portrait of Coco (L. D. Gaboriaux Collection, Paris)

Edgar Degas: Woman with Chrysanthemums (1865, Metropolitan Museum of Art, New York)

EDGAR DEGAS: Dancer Bowing to the Audience (Louvre, Paris)

nudes, half-length nudes, and seated nudes, all with undefined backgrounds. To him, form was 'frozen rhythm' movement characterised by flowing, elongated lines which develop into curves. They express the acute, elegant sensibility of the artist who took refuge from the realistic truth of the object and retired into his inner self (Brizio), where everything was transposed into fantasy. His colours were beautiful and simple, like those of enamel; he gave no depth, and modulated colour in a way that had nothing in common with the earlier search for chiaroscuro or tonalities.

There are many versions of some of his works. In all of them the prevalent note is one of ecstasy and at the same time melancholy, which were the dominant notes in Modigliani's tragic life.

Towards the end of the nineteenth and the beginning of the twentieth century, other Italian painters lived and worked in Paris. Among the first group were Giuseppe De Nittis, Giovanni Boldini, Federico Zandomeneghi. While still at home they had expressed Italian art in a vital manner; in France they became even more vital, but reverted after their return to Italy to their former way of painting. In the second group were De Chirico, Carrà, Morandi, Sironi and others.

Giorgio De Chirico (1888—   ), attracted by German Romanticism, showed, at the beginning of his career, a similarity to Böcklin in choice of subject and figures, but De Chirico's intimacy of concept, his suggestion of a bygone epoch, his way of relating dream episodes intermingled with a certain intellectual irony, suspense and anguish (Valsecchi), eventually emerged as Metaphysical painting. One may say that these tins, biscuits, rubber-gloves and dummies, when seen from an ironic or anguished point of view, transport the onlooker to a bewitched, delirious world frozen into immobility.

Carlo Carrà (1881—   ) was among those who signed the Manifesto of the Futurist Painters drafted by Umberto Boccioni in 1910. Giacomo Balla (1871—   ) and Gino Severini (1883—   ) also belonged to this group. From a militant Futurism of decomposed tangled design (see his *Portrait of Marinetti*), Carrà turned to more moderate landscapes and figures. Yet in spite of Cézanne's Cubist influence, Carrà should be looked upon as a creator of Futurism—that Italian-born, formal manner of painting.

Giorgio Morandi (1890—   ), though not ignorant of Carrà's and De Chirico's forms and metaphysics, stands apart from them. He does not attempt to evoke an enchanted atmosphere and abstruse figure combinations, but 'tries to find what may be called a pure geometric order: cylinders, cubes, spheroids and bottles are set on planes swept by rays of light,' in a perspective which may have been inspired by Piero della Francesca.

Mario Sironi (1885—   ) also had Metaphysical leanings. His colours—particularly compared to Campigli's and Casorati's—may be called shrill; Cubist tendencies are just hinted at, but Matisse seems to be ever-present in these paintings.

IX

At the beginning of this century Henri Matisse became—perhaps involuntarily—the centre of the Fauves, 'the wild beasts'. They exhibited in Paris, first at the gallery of Berthe Weill, later at the Salon des Indépendants.

If for nothing else, these exhibitions would be memorable for the names of the artists who took part in them: Derain, Vlaminck, Dufy, Rouault, Marquet, Jean Puy, Kees van Dongen, Othon Friesz and other fanatics of colour. Some of them were, like Matisse, pupils of Moreau, who, as a member of the Academy, and Elie Delaunay's successor at the Ecole des Beaux-Arts, would have liked his pupils to paint mythological subjects and to observe orthodox rules. But it is probable that Moreau did not force any rules on his pupils, and, being himself an intellectual and imaginative, he may even have encouraged them to experiment.

This new movement was followed by another, Cubism. The basis of Cubism was and is critical analysis of the artists' own sentiments (and, therefore, of the object to be represented). Cézanne propounded this with such energy, as he himself put it, to counteract the 'soft' self-indulgence of Impressionism. Thus representation of Nature was reduced to strict stereometric formulas; from it first followed Analytical Cubism and, later, Synthetic Cubism. Fauvism identified colour with the object itself, which means that colour is not 'the accidental appearance of the object' but, speaking from the painter's point of view, its very essence. Thus, here are two parallel movements and theories—Cubism based on form, Fauvism, on colour.

Henri Matisse (1869—1954) was the titular head of the Fauvist movement, though he really preferred to keep outside the circle. As a Fauve he stimulated Fauvism outside France.

'What I should like to achieve above anything,' said Matisse, 'is expression.' But in saying this he wanted to justify the violence with which artists now ignored technical means and, stressing dramatic subjectivity, even stretching it to the grotesque, disrupted the balance.

Thus Expressionism became another typical manifestation of a 'Romantic attitude of the spirit', and without control gave itself up to its own torment. This would apply more correctly to the later champions of the movement than to Matisse himself. In 1928 when the *Red Odalisque* was painted the critics accused him of being influenced by Japanese prints and oriental miniatures. This and *Blue Eyes*, of 1935, were far removed from Fauvism.

Matisse died at the age of eighty-five. He was only thirty when he made his first impact with *Countryside Round Toulouse*; this was followed by such paintings as *Head of an Italian* (1901), *Carmelina* (1903), *Young Sailor* (1906), *Women by the Sea-shore* (1908), and *Spanish Girl* (1909). He at one time tried his hand at Pointillism, but he soon returned to his technique of pure colours, to his orchestra-like compositions (Diehl) and to his somewhat severe but brilliant lyricism.

His paintings are always in keeping with the theories he had created; they seem belong to four periods, into which his working life may be divided, namely: the Art of Expression, the Art of Emancipation, the Art of Harmony, the Art of Balance, Calm and Purity. So his development continued from *Tree in the Countryside near Triveaux* to *Nude on a Settee*, and many other nudes, innumerable still-lifes, flowers, goldfish, portraits and decorative figures to the grandeur of the famous *Branch of a Plum Tree on an Ochre Background* (1948). In that same year there was a one-man show of two hundred and seventy-one of his paintings at the Philadelphia Museum of Art. He went on indefatigably. In 1950 he painted the *St Dominic* for a Church at Assy, while his one-man show was making a triumphant progress across the United States from New York to Cleveland, Chicago and San Francisco. He designed the Rosary Chapel for the Dominican Sisters of Vence and painted the walls himself. The figure of the Spanish saint with its contours more in graffito than in painting, and only just discernible, covers a whole wall. The huge figure, deep in prayer, seems outside the realm of reality and reason.

In the field of ecclesiastic Art Matisse also did some magnificent church windows. A series of his lofty engravings is at the Library of Art and Archaeology of Paris University.

Georges Braque (1882—   ) worked from 1908 onwards according to the principles of Cézanne whose aim it had been to find a common denominator, as it were, for reality. One may say, however, that Picasso came nearer to this principle: Picasso, who dissolved form to re-compose it so that to the eye of the artist the picture gains a new reality. He created an architecture in which 'space is anti-realistic yet compelling by the varied arrangement of planes which together convey the feeling of space.' This was later to corrupt (some would say complete) Cubism to the point of incorporating foreign material such as printed words, newspaper cuttings, even multicoloured bits of paper or rags into the picture (collage) 'to render the proper colour of objects without the use of a paint-brush.' Braque, it is true, when applying Cubist techniques achieved limpid harmonies; he was especially preoccupied with representing in the same picture figures and objects in their various inner and outer aspects. It became an Orphic art which Apollinaire called 'the art of representing pictures with the help of new elements which do not belong to the visual world but are created within the artist's mind and endowed by him with complete reality.' This 'pure' art to which Léger, Picabia, Marcel Duchamp, the Czech Frantisek Kupka and the Russian Sonia Terk were irresistibly drawn, developed into an art of despair which without real motifs achieved its effects by using spectral refraction to create geometrical forms. Robert Delaunay caught some of that despair when he said: 'No horizontals, no verticals; light deforms and decomposes everything.' Thus Delaunay's pictures became veritable rainbow-fragments (Reid).

The art of our days which meets with so much interest, enthusiasm and perplexity had a span of fifty years to develop, so we are not dealing with improvisation. Modern art may be traced back to many influences; one thing is certain, however: that well before the First World War important things had happened in the field of art.

In nearly all European countries society lived through a state of crisis, then as yet unknown to them. This malaise, whose roots undoubtedly were political, had a profound effect on the arts.

Henri de Toulouse-Lautrec: Woman Combing her Hair (water-colour)

The young artists, who could no longer bear the intellectualism of a decadent epoch, tried to counteract it by a faith in a new world. Röthel, who wrote the history of the German groups of artists *Die Brücke* and the *Blaue Reiter*—which together formed the *Wilden*, the counterpart of the French Fauves—thought that that world was Nietzsche's world, in which 'the beautiful, the unknown, the problematic, the terrible and the divine were abundant.' It was the yet unknown world of Zarathustra that was to build the 'altars for the new religion of the spirit.' Matisse's statement that what he wanted to achieve above all was expression was taken over by the German *Wilden* without the restraint and the *esprit* of the French Fauves (Röthel).

Among these various movements, the Italian Futurists proved themselves as extremists: anti-Impressionist reaction did not seem enough for them; they jumped intermediary stages and did not dabble in Expressionism. Their pursuits (which were also fruitful outside the province of art) were above theories and systems.

From the Munich 'Latin Quarter,' *Schwabing*, came some innovators, first among them Ludwig Kirchner. They attracted public attention with their novel ideas and tempestuous ways. Their herald was the ever-argumentative group the *Blaue Reiter*. The focal point of German Expressionism, however, was Dresden and its circle of artists called *Die Brücke* (1905—1913). As is the way with communities based on sentiment (Röthel) there was something of the esoteric, of black magic about them. The motto of these artists, who under the flag of anarchism undeniably professed Romantic idealism, was *Odi profanum vulgus*. This new German Expressionism began with Paula Modersohn-Becker (1876—1907) who still adhered to the true image of Nature, and continued with the colouristic dreams of Ernst Wilhelm Nay, the abstract Expressionist, who created free harmonies of colour which did not lack a certain rhythm. This Expressionistic movement was to give the lead to a number of other painters who, though of varied standing, had all had good training.

PAUL CÉZANNE: Still-life (National Gallery of Art, Washington) →

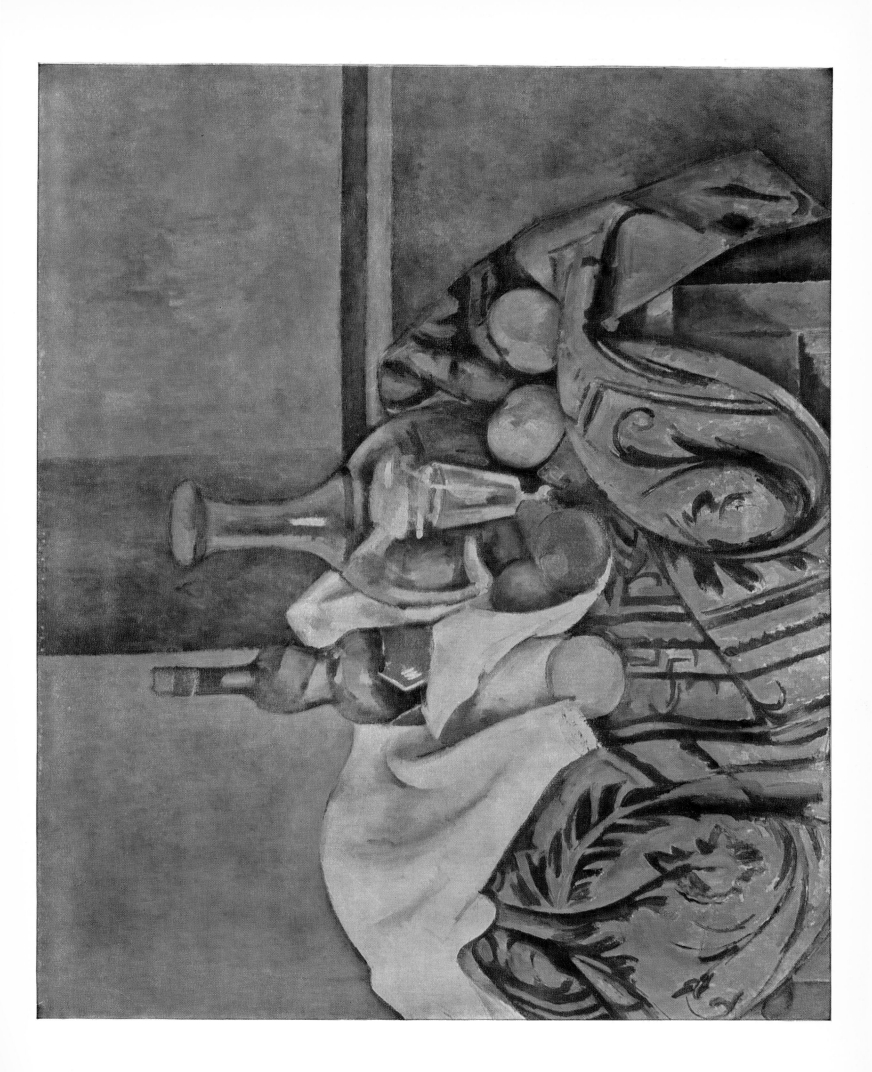

HENRI DE TOULOUSE-LAUTREC: Girl of the 'House' (Toulouse-Lautrec Museum, Albi)

· PAUL CÉZANNE: Vase of Flowers (National Gallery of Art, Washington) →

HENRI DE TOULOUSE-LAUTREC: Housewife (pencil drawing)

← BERTHE MORISOT: Cherry Picking (Private Collection, Paris)

PAUL CÉZANNE: Still-life (water-colour)

When was German Expressionism born? We know *Die Brücke*, the *Blaue Reiter*, and some of its surrealistic relations very well, but we must not forget the forerunners such as Christian Rohlfs, Ferdinand Hodler, James Ensor, Alexei von Jawlensky, Edvard Munch, Wassily Kandinsky, Emil Nolde and Ernst Barlach, who, in good time, joined the movement and took part in its controversies more or less officially.

These were the 'Gothic men' who thought that classical interpretation of the organic world with its serene surroundings as a background for man was no longer the answer to the exigencies to which the art of Northern and Central Europe was able to give expression (Worringer). They felt impregnated with that mysterious pathos which wanted to enliven 'inorganic' Nature (Reid).

These 'Gothic men' were not all German born. Among them were Belgians (van Dongen), Swiss (Amiet, Klee), Finns (Gallén-Kallela), Russians (Kandinsky, Chagall), but whatever their country of origin they were all baptised with the waters of the Seine. Rouault, Picabia, Delaunay, Utrillo, Derain and Vlaminck lived in Paris. Between 1900 and 1904 Braque, Léger, Arp and Duchamp had moved there from the French provinces. They were joined by Brancusi, Carrà, Boccioni, Severini, Modigliani, Klee, Juan Gris, Archipenko, Chagall, Kandinsky, Naum Gabo, Jawlensky, Paula Modersohn-Becker, Nolde and Franz Marc. Picasso, who first came to Paris in 1900, did not settle there till later. Impressionism and Neo-Impressionism were not dead yet, and neither were Fauvism and Cubism. Futurism with Balla, Russolo and Boccioni as its representatives 'advocated any form of originality, however audacious and violent it might be.' These Futurist painters tried to instil courage and self-assurance into their colleagues 'even when faced with being

PAUL CÉZANNE: Self-portrait (lithograph)

VINCENT VAN GOGH: Portrait of Doctor Gachet (etching)

PIERRE AUGUSTE RENOIR: The Swing (Louvre, Paris)

PAUL CÉZANNE: Three Women Bathing (Petit Palais, Paris)

PAUL CÉZANNE: Madame Cézanne in the Garden (Stephen C. Clark Collection, New York) →

VINCENT VAN GOGH: Self-portrait (1887, V. W. van Gogh Collection, Amsterdam)

reproached with madness.' The Manifesto of the Futurist Painters of February 11th, 1910, declared itself against paintings in the nude, which they thought 'just as debasing as writing about adultery.'

Along with these phenomena, decadent art, the heritage of Romanticism, began to appear, bringing with it not only elegance and refinement but as their reverse side a desperate taste for vice, and rebellion against every moral code (Oscar Wilde's *Picture of Dorian Gray*), a way of looking upon art as a means of evading everyday life (as in Wagner's *Tristan and Isolde* and in the writings of Baudelaire, Verlaine and Mallarmé). At this time an Italian movement—the so-called 'Crepuscularism'—made itself felt. It wanted to end high-sounding rhetorics, and it asked the artists to turn to the small things and ordinary feelings of everyday life. This art was soon found to be unsatisfactory and the loss of the 'great passions and conceptions which were now not to be expressed' was lamented. After the First World War they were to come back in a sinister way.

In the stormy climate of Europe before 1914, artists everywhere acquired the same language as the Dresden and Munich groups. They were all equally confused, torn by the same conflicts of ideas and temperament.

← PAUL CÉZANNE: Thatched Cottages at Auvers (George Renand Collection, Paris)

VINCENT VAN GOGH: Portrait of a Peasant (pen-and-reed)

PAUL GAUGUIN: Women of Martinique (pastel)

Some of the German artists were but mediocre and imitative, but there were also a great many talented ones. Were they all Expressionist without any longing for the past? Without looking back or straying from their chosen path? Were not some of them carried over the border-line of Breton's communistic Surrealism into abstract painting? Were they purely painters, or were they painters and theorists? Or even theorists who happened to be painters also and who wanted to apply their theories?

Otto Mueller (1874—1930) had been a craftsman, a lithographer and wood-engraver before he took to painting. He had a leaning towards the archaic. Schmidt-Rottluff and Kirchner, the one a vigorous, the other an impulsive painter, had been his teachers.

Ernst Ludwig Kirchner (1880—1938)—together with Heckel and Pechstein—was the founder of *Die Brücke*. All three were at that time about twenty-five. Kirchner proclaimed the 'inner intuition' (a phrase coined by him). By that he meant that the true substance of reality was not so much in the image of the external world as in the image which the world of feeling evoked in the artist's mind. This was borne out in his *Self-portrait* (Karlsruhe), in *Dancing Classes* (Private Collection, Düsseldorf), and in *Alpine Hut* (Karlsruhe).

Though it would be wrong to say that Schmidt-Rottluff (1884—   ) painted in exactly the same manner as Kirchner, he used a similar palette, as can be seen in *Self-portrait* (Moeller Gallery, Cologne) and *Mediterranean Port* (Bekker vom Rath Collection, Hofheim). Schmidt-Rottluff travelled widely and was an industrious painter. In 1936 he was banned by the Nazis and excluded from exhibitions. Will Grohmann wrote a comprehensive monograph (with bibliography) on him, published in Stuttgart in 1956 under the title: *Karl Schmidt-Rottluff*.

PAUL GAUGUIN: Still-life (detail)
(1889, Brown-Bovery Collection, Baden,
Switzerland)

The Nazis also condemned Erich Heckel (1883—   ), whose art they accused of being decadent.   When
still young, Heckel painted *Reclining Girl*, a nude (1909, Bavarian State Galleries), and *Clear Day* (*Gläserner
Tag*) (1912, Kruss Collection, Berlin).   His painting is reminiscent of Fauvism, yet in the simplification of
the plastic form (not in composition) he touches on Gauguin.   His characteristics are a stirring inspiration,
an impetuous fantasy and a rapid execution.

Oskar Kokoschka was born in 1886 in Austria, but he also lived and worked in Germany, England and
the Near East.   There is a portrait of his of the *Poet Dirsztay* (1910) in which a merciless analysis seems to
reveal the character of the sitter.   He experimented with Expressionism and always arrived at 'a tangible
solution'.   A *Portrait of Mrs Nancy Cunard* (1924, Bienert Collection, Munich) also indicates his deep psychological insight.   In the same year there was a view of Venice, showing the city dreaming beyond the agitated
waters of the Lagoon (Bavarian State Galleries, Munich).

August Macke (1887—1914), another important figure in modern German art, was much engrossed in
controversy with his colleagues who did not acknowledge the *Blaue Reiter*.   Some of his writings appeared
under the title *The Masks*.   He exhibited in many shows in Munich, Bonn and Cologne, then exiled himself
to Switzerland, worked there for many months at the Thuner-See and in 1914 went, together with Klee and
Moilliet, to Tunisia.   War broke out.   He joined the army and was killed at Perthes on September 26th.
Macke may have had a foreboding of his death.   In a series of woodcuts which he left behind, there is one

CAMILLE PISSARRO: Peasant Woman (Private Collection, New York)   →

124

GEORGES SEURAT: The Jockey (Private Collection, Paris)

Henri de Toulouse-Lautrec: Spanish Riding School (Knoedler Gallery, New York)

Paul Gauguin: Noa-Noa (wood engraving)

←   Pierre Auguste Renoir: Young Girl with Cat (1885, Chester Dale Collection, National Gallery of Art, Washington)

GEORGES SEURAT: Study (charcoal drawing)

ANDRÉ DUNOYER DE SEGONZAC: Woman with Arms Folded (etching)

ALBERT MARQUET: The Harbour at Naples (India ink drawing)

—*Departure*—which shows the minute figure of a man in the nude on horseback saluting with broad gestures three other figures. The black and white of this woodcut may not be without symbolic meaning. Of his paintings we should like to mention the *Walk on the Bridge* and the little *Turkish Café* (1914).

Franz Marc (1880—1916) was a close friend of Macke, with whom at one time he had visited Delaunay. Like Macke, he was killed in the war (at Verdun).

Marc was a complex figure. It may be some help towards understanding what he was aiming at in his painting if one knows that he was preoccupied with philosophical and theological studies. This would also explain an at times missionary-like attitude of his. After having left the *Neue Künstlervereinigung*, he became one of the founders of the *Blaue Reiter*. There he attained the position which he deserved by virtue of his talent and by the enthusiasm of his writings. He first exhibited in Munich and then, in 1913, at the *Erste Deutsche Herbstsalon* (First German Autumn Salon). Some of his works are: the *Large Blue Horses* (1911, Walker Art Center, Minneapolis); a drawing in tempera, *Two Horses* (Rhode Island School of Design, Providence); a canvas *Tyrol* in the same Munich Museum as are Marc's woodcuts (mostly of animals: tigers and foals).

Also among German artists who deserve a place in modern painting are Feininger, Corinth and Beckmann. Lyonel Feininger (1871—1956) was born in New York. His works are experiments in 'dense harmonious colour, their themes mostly the sea and boats: near-abstractions of spacious luminosity.' A picture such as the dynamic *Cyclists* (1912) calls to mind Futurist painting. Lovis Corinth (1858—1925) and Max Slevogt (1868—1932), both stemming from Impressionism, belonged to the Munich *Sezession*. Max Beckmann (1884—1950) went to Amsterdam in 1933 and after the war to the United States. 'Of a precocious talent,' he

Paul Cézanne: The Blue Vase (1885-87, Louvre, Paris)

GEORGES SEURAT: The Models (1887-88, Barnes Foundation, Merion, Pennsylvania)

GEORGES SEURAT: The Bridge at Courbevoie (1886, Courtauld Institute, London)

VINCENT VAN GOGH: The Postman Roulin (1888, Museum of Fine Arts, Boston)

VINCENT VAN GOGH: Road with Cypresses (1890, Kröller-Müller Museum, Otterlo)

PAUL GAUGUIN: La Belle Angèle (1889, Jeu de Paume, Paris)

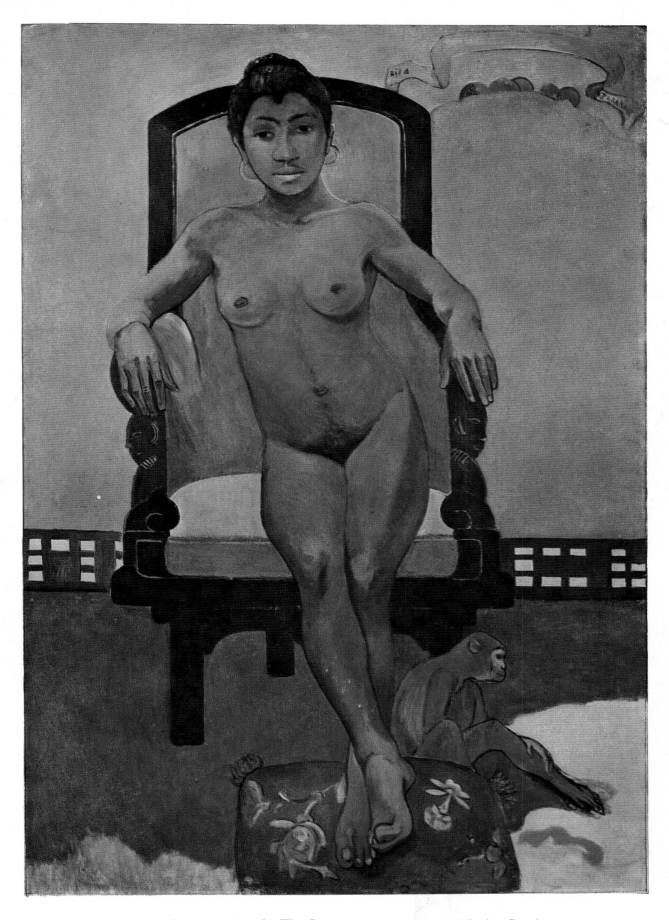

PAUL GAUGUIN: Annah, The Javanese (1893, Hahnloser Collection, Berne)

PIERRE BONNARD: The Breakfast (c. 1907, Petit Palais, Paris)

ODILON REDON: Mlle Violette H. (1899, Cleveland Museum of Art, U. S. A.)

HENRI ROUSSEAU: The Snake Charmer (1907, Musée d'Art Moderne, Paris)

VINCENT VAN GOGH: Self-portrait (detail) →
(1889, Private Collection, New York)

GEORGES BRAQUE: Anemones (1925, Private Collection, New York)

←   HENRI DE TOULOUSE-LAUTREC: M. Dethomas at the Opera
(Private Collection, New York)

RAOUL DUFY: Landscape (1939, Private Collection, Paris)

André Derain: The Wood (1920, Musée d'Art Moderne, Paris)

Maurice Utrillo: Café 'Point de Vue' (1922, Galerie Bernheim Jeune, Paris)

LOVIS CORINTH: Walchensee (1924, Bavarian State Galleries, Munich)

JUAN GRIS: Still-life with Bordeaux Bottle (1919, T. and A. Werner Collection, Berlin)

Lyonel Feininger: Market Church at Halle (1930, Bavarian State Galleries, Munich)

FRANZ MARC: Tyrol (1913-14, Bavarian State Galleries, Munich)

Max Beckmann: Self-portrait (1944, Bavarian State Galleries, Munich)

MARC CHAGALL: The Bridal Couple (1930, Le Roy Berdeau Collection, Palm Beach, Florida)

PAUL KLEE: Before the Snow (1929, Private Collection, Berne)

André Dunoyer de Segonzac: Landscape near Moret (1938, George Levy Collection, Paris)

← Georges Rouault: Crucifix
(1932, White Collection, Ardmore, Pennsylvania)

157

EDOUARD VUILLARD: La Lecture (1939, Private Collection, Paris)

ALBERT MARQUET: Landscape in Algeria (1938, Private Collection, Paris)

HENRI ROUSSEAU: Sleeping Gipsy (1897, Museum of Modern Art, New York)

PABLO PICASSO: The Studio (1935, Musée d'Art Moderne, Paris)

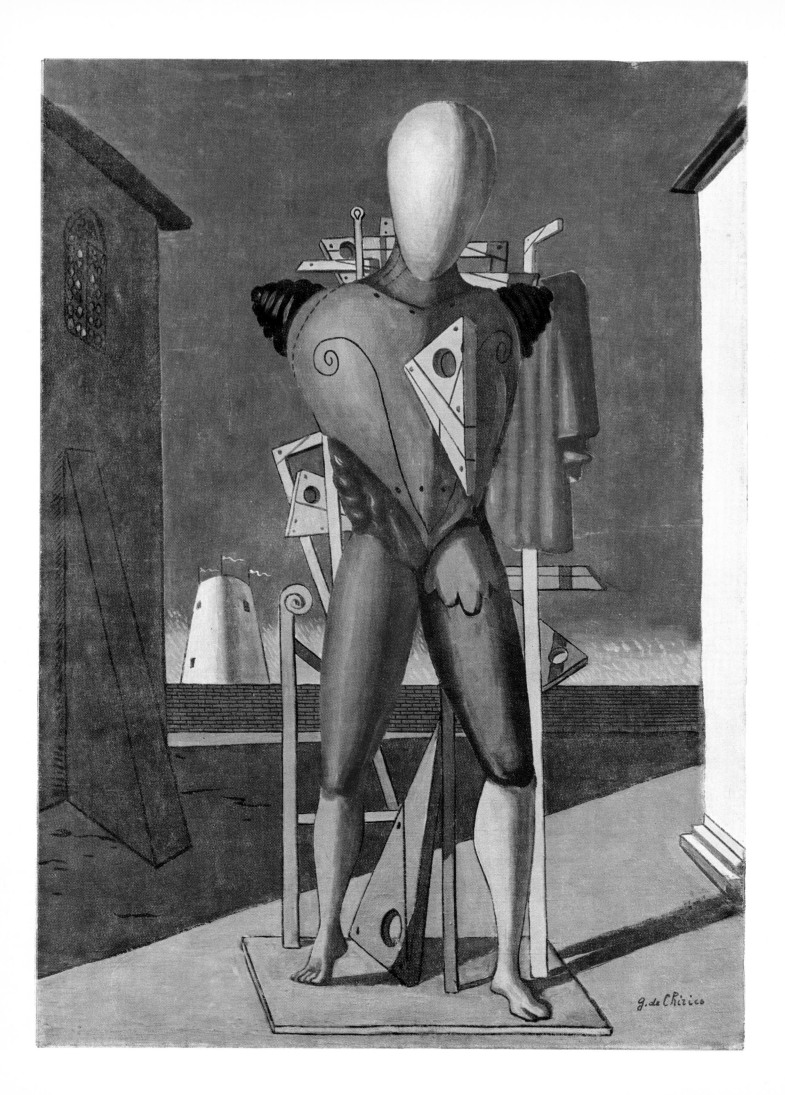

GIORGIO MORANDI: Large Metaphysical Still-life (1918, Dr Emilio Jesi Collection, Milan)

←
GIORGIO DE CHIRICO: Hector's Return
(1917, Private Collection, Milan)

ERICH HECKEL: Clear Day (Gläserner Tag) (1912, Markus Kinn Collection, Berlin)

ERNST LUDWIG KIRCHNER: Alpine Hut (1917, Staatliche Kunsthalle, Karlsruhe)

OTTO MUELLER: Gipsies (c. 1925, Private Collection)

OSKAR KOKOSCHKA: Portrait of Mrs Nancy Cunard (1924, Bienert Collection, Munich)

WASSILY KANDINSKY: Improvisation (1910, Art Gallery, Yale University, New Haven, Connecticut)

MAX LIEBERMANN: Street Scene (charcoal drawing)

first showed leanings towards the Impressionism of the Leipzig School and later studied in Weimar, Paris and Florence. 'He had taken an active part in the intense cultural life of pre-Nazi Germany. The result of his experiences of that time was a definite realistic attitude which pledged him to works of solid construction and unerring choice of colour,' as is borne out in many pictures, such as the *Black Lily*, the triptych *Departure*, the *Argonauts, Roulette, The Boat*, the Munich *Self-portrait*, and a series of lithographs, *Inferno*, which first drew attention to him.

Although one admires him as a painter, his theories seem somewhat strange: 'My painting is based on the constructive rhythm of the Cabbala, while my thoughts wander from Oanes Dagon to the last days of submerged continents.' (*Meine Theorie der Malerei*, a lecture delivered on July 21st, 1938, at the New Burlington Gallery, London.)

It would be difficult to say who of the Munich or Dresden Group, or for that matter who of any other foreign groups which had sprung up inspired by these two, was dominant during the last years preceding the First World War. These groups mostly disintegrated during the War. But one of the undoubted masters of that period was Paul Klee (1879—1940), a German born in Berne. At times he was diverted from the abstract (towards which he had definite leanings). He was indefatigable both as a painter and a teacher. Klee, the theorist, laid down the rules for the values of form. 'Colour,' he stated, 'means firstly " quality ", secondly " weight ", because it has not only colouristic value, but also luminosity. Thirdly " measure ", because (apart from the above-mentioned qualities) it defines limits, contours and extension and therefore is measurable.'

Klee was a lecturer at the Düsseldorf Academy and also at the Bauhaus, where he influenced many later painters. Apart from him there were many teachers through whose influence modern art has spread.

Otto Mueller was a teacher at the Breslau Academy; Kanoldt, also at Breslau, and in Berlin; Schlemmer in Wuppertal; Beckmann, in New York; Pechstein, Hofer and Schmidt-Rottluff, in Berlin; Feininger at Mills College, California.

Closely connected with the development of German Expressionist painting is Breton's surrealistic, 'purely physical automatism.' Two painters who, free from any aesthetic or moral restrictions, were driven solely by the impulses which they received, unchecked by reason, were the Russians Wassily Kandinsky (1866—1944), from Moscow, and Marc Chagall (1887—   ), from Vitebsk.

Kandinsky was the main exponent of that abstract movement which was curbed and nearly annihilated by the events of the 1914—1918 War. It came to life once more with the Weimar and Dessau Bauhaus under Gropius' direction. The old ideals of the *Blaue Reiter* were now realised: the aim of abstract art—to express the mind of man—was developed; abstract painting proper, i.e. the non-objective musical construction in pure colours and lines, was achieved (Formaggio).

Kandinsky painted in the abstract manner from 1910 onwards; in that year he produced a water-colour which may be called the first non-objective work of art in our time, and, as such, caused a sensation. Other works such as the great *Compositions* followed: their wealth of rhythm seems 'like music transposed into colour.'

Chagall, on the other hand, painted his memories of his country even though it seemed to have forgotten him. He also did book illustrations. His brush-strokes and colours are, one may say, dreamy; his pictures are of huts and muzhiks, and of folk-lore. Memorable among them are *Cockerel and Harlequin* (1928) and the *Fall of the Angel* (1923). He has leanings towards Cubism, yet is no Cubist; one could, with just as much justification, call him Expressionist or Surrealist (Formaggio). But he really goes his own way, and as he is preoccupied with the human figure one cannot call him a non-objective painter.

The nature and limitations of this volume do not allow for even a moderately comprehensive history of modern painting. Yet Juan Gris (1887—1927), together with Delaunay, Léger, Gleizes and Braque, went along with Picasso on his first experiments. André Derain (1880—1954), by means similar to those of Vlaminck, movingly expressed vital, earthbound forces at work (Sedlmayr). Both Derain and Vlaminck can, in spite of their different ways of experimenting, be traced back to Fauvism, with some Cubistic and neo-Gothic elements added in Derain's work. Among Derain's works are: *Collioure* (private collection, United States), *Figure in a Field* (private collection, Paris), *Le Pont de Pâques* (1910, Museum for Modern Western Art, Moscow), *Saturday* (1914, Museum for Modern Western Art, Moscow), *Harlequin and Pierrot* (1924), the *Hunt* (1928).

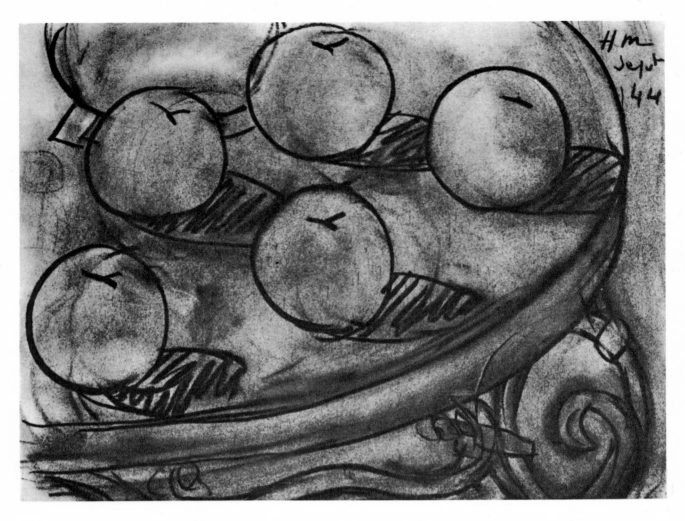

HENRI MATISSE: Apples on a Table (pencil drawing)

Vlaminck's works include: the *Flood, Ivry, La Maison à l'Auvent* (Museum of Modern Art, Paris) and a *Self-portrait*.

In speaking of the artistic revolution which broke out with Expressionism and has not yet come to an end, Georges Rouault (1871—1958) should be mentioned as one of its eminent figures. In his early work he either contorted the objects in his paintings or made himself independent of them; they were full of 'religious fears, a longing for redemption, the inherent pathos of colour, the debasement of man,' as represented in his well-known clowns, criminals and prostitutes; then, in a graphic series such as *Miserere*, he turned to religious subjects—to the *Redeemer*, to *Saints* and to those *Legendary Landscapes* of 'magnificent forms and delightfully transparent colour.' Of his early works we should like to mention: the *Dead Christ* (1895), the *Builder's Yard* (1897), the *Apprentice, Suburban Landscape* and the *Tightrope Walker*. Tightrope walkers were a subject by which Rouault seems to have been obsessed; what attracted him there was the element of sadness. Their roving life seemed to him like the artist's life. He painted the essence of their very being, depicted them from the human side and was almost overawed by them. His *Crucifixion*, on the other hand, does not show as much piety as adoration. Venturi has this to say about it: 'The Old Masters put the cross in their pictures to give them a monumental effect—not so Rouault. With him the figure of Christ rises from the ground, and what gives the figure its monumental effect is the broad torso and the raised head; He is the King and the Redeemer who seems to open His arms wide to protect the faithful.'

It is impossible in the scope of this volume to refer to any but the most outstanding or the eccentric, and Salvador Dali (1904—   ), a surrealist who stands out by his 'Baroque boldness', belongs to the latter.

HENRI MATISSE: Woman with
Anemones (1937, Paul Rosenberg
Collection, Paris)

In choice of theme he imitated De Chirico and others, yet some of his theories were novel and his execution,
though lacking in seriousness, skilful. In his religious paintings, such as the *Virgin* and *Pietà*, he seems to
have come to terms with his mystical Surrealism.

Together with him, we should mention some Expressionist artists who became Dadaist or Surrealist painters:
Marcel Duchamp, Francis Picabia, Joan Miró, Max Ernst and Yves Tanguy... but now we come to the
greatest exponent of contemporary painting—Picasso.

Pablo Picasso (1881—   ) is 'an adventurer of genius'; if this may sound like condemnation to some,
it is really high praise for this 'bold, experimenting' mind and the work it produces.

Picasso, to be precise, did not invent Cubism, which was pioneered by Cézanne. In 1906 he painted his
series the *Tightrope Walkers*. Before that a Lithuanian—Tschurlianis (sometimes spelt Zurlianis)—had painted
a picture which lays claim to be 'the first painting devoid of any relationship to reality.'

Before Picasso had entered the scene Cubism had only been in its infancy. With Picasso's *Demoiselles
d'Avignon* (1906-1907) it burst upon the scene. It was followed in 1910 by *Girl with Mandolin* and by *Woman
from Arles* (1911). Soon after the First World War a gentler Picasso reappeared with some versions of the
theme *Mother and Child* and various portraits of his son. These were all formal and sedate. After about
1925 he went through a phase of violent Expressionism which reached its peak in 1932 with *Bathers Playing
Ball* and many studies of reclining nudes.

Guernica (1937) seems the key to Picasso's change of front. 'He is now intent on denouncing the mon-
strous and oppressive forms of our civilisation,' as he does later in *Seated Woman, Bulls' Heads*, etc. *Massacre
in Korea* (1951) recalls in spirit and expression the oppressive atmosphere and anxiety which his fellow-national

172

ALEXEI VON JAWLENSKY: Landscape near Murnau (1912, Bekker vom Rath Collection, Hofheim)

HENRI MATISSE: Splendour, Complacency and Lust (1907-08, Statens Museum for Art, Copenhagen)

Henri Matisse: Flowers and Ceramic Plate (1911, Le Roy Berdeau Collection, Palm Beach, Florida)

EDVARD MUNCH: Girls on a Bridge (1906, Wallraf-Richartz Museum, Cologne)

PIERRE BONNARD: Portrait of a Woman (study) (charcoal drawing)

MAURICE UTRILLO: The Banks of the Seine, Paris (lithograph)

and predecessor Goya had put into his paintings, stemming as it were, from the same apocalyptic conception. But there are more facets to Picasso's mind. In his female nudes and in his robots he repeats in a modern vein what Goya had expressed in his *Executions of the Third of May* (Shooting of the Madrid Rebels). His Pastoral scenes, his *Women Reading*, his landscapes, such as *View of Vallauris*, reflect an altogether different mood, and to counteract the desperation of the *Massacre* he creates *War* and *Peace*, 'images of a world which has lost its humanity.'

Perhaps Picasso's mind is one of changing moods, but, with the Expressionists, change of mood has lost its meaning. They talk only about an 'aesthetic man' or an 'interesting artist' of, one may say, Kierkegaard-like Existentialism. The same applies to 'style,' but neither mood nor style seems to apply to Picasso, who on the one hand painted an Impressionistic nude, *Girl with Basket of Flowers*, and on the other *Woman with Tambourine*, done in a perfunctory manner that would have horrified his father, who was a teacher of design. Yet in the *Woman with Tambourine* a new trend towards constructive principles may be detected.

Picasso's problem is now no longer to represent man or woman, or to convey an ephemeral effect of colour and light, 'but to give to the one-dimensional surface of the canvas a geometrical feeling of three-dimensionality in which forms themselves were in continuous rapport with their disposition in space.' Sometimes even these forms are absent; this would have pleased Apollinaire, the prophet of all styles which had followed after Impressionism. 'Too long,' he said, 'have we worshipped man, animals, plants and stars; the time has come to show them that we are the masters...'

So Picasso in his work represents nothing else but the 'aesthetic man'. He is the incarnation of a perfect taste with a turn towards the piquant and the surprising. Sedlmayr has this to say about him: 'In Picasso

PABLO PICASSO: Study (red chalk and pen-and-reed drawing)

PABLO PICASSO: Still-life (1924, Private Collection)

we see the personification of the most radical of *quodlibetarius* of the *peregrinus proteus*.' He is capable of transforming himself into anything, 'now into God, now into a grain of sand.' He embodies aestheticism to the ultimate and, through the medium of his personality, in doing so reveals its very essence.

Picasso is reproached with many things, among them his ideological trend towards the Left, and his scepticism as an artist. Pertinent to this there is in the *Cahiers d'Art* of 1935 a quotation of a talk between Picasso and Zervos: 'To me,' says Picasso, 'a picture is the sum total of so many destructive processes. It is neither planned nor preconceived right through from the beginning; it changes along with the changing attitude of the painter while working on it.'

The last generation of painters moved from Matisse towards Picasso, who in his own way solved the problem of the synthetic fusion between the 'results of Cubism, the riotous colour of Expressionism and the constructive teachings of abstract art.' At the moment a plethora of artists all over Europe prove that there are many bold tendencies at work: an exuberance of colour, Rayonism, Suprematism, Non-objective art, Constructivism—movements more or less ephemeral which chase each other and because of their very transience act as aesthetic and cultural ferments with remarkable repercussions.

X

Most of the French contemporary artists are grouped together in the 'School of Paris' if school one can call it. It is certainly not a school in the old sense of Barbizon, of Worpswede or of Laethem-St Martin.

CARLO CARRÀ: Still-life (1916, Frua Collection, Milan)   →

OSKAR SCHLEMMER: Group at the Balustrade (1913, Bienert Collection, Munich)

AUGUST MACKE: Sailing Boats (1910, Mr and Mrs Sigmund Heumann Collection, New York)

MARC CHAGALL: Soldier Drinking (1912, Museum of Modern Art, New York)

PABLO PICASSO: The Drinkers (etching)

PABLO PICASSO: Girl with Basket of Flowers
(detail) (1905)

As Marcel Brion says: 'The name " School of Paris " has no real significance, as in our days the pictorial vocabulary—particularly as regards abstract art—has become so much more international and universal. Artists of the last two generations speak, as it were, the same language, preserving their own individuality, but expressing it now in a world-wide style: from Milan to San Francisco, from London to Buenos Aires, from Berlin to Tokyo.' All the same, the contact of artists of such diverse nationalities as represented in the School of Paris leads to an exchange of various aesthetic theories and hence to mutual influence.

We have mentioned earlier some Belgian artists. At the beginning of the nineteenth century, Belgian painting, with Navez at its head, had not been insensitive to Ingres' and David's teaching. Soon afterwards Gustav Wappers, an historical painter, had become the main exponent of Romanticism. Around him a number of painters collected: De Keyser from Antwerp, Gallait from Tournai, Wiertz from Dinant and Leys (1815—1867); Leys was of the French School of Fermois and was a landscape painter of quality. The reaction of the French against Naturalism spurred on the Belgians; from among them emerged such personalities as Lievin de Winne, Florent Willems (reminiscent of the old Dutch masters of interiors), de Groux, and Louis Dubois, whose choice of subjects calls to mind Millet and Courbet, the painter of animals Joseph Stevens, landscape painters like Boulenger, Verwee, Wauters and finally eminent engravers like Rops. The ' Circle of the Twenty' was the focus of Belgian Impressionism. We have already mentioned Ensor, but there are others to add to this list of Belgian artists: Theo van Risselberghe (1862—1926), Ferdinand Khnopff (1858—1921), Vogels, Lemmen and Donnay. A second movement which reflected the artistic exigencies of the period was *Libre Esthétique* to which belonged Groux, Eymaus, Frédéric, Laermans and Claus.

A group called *Young Belgian Painting* represented the avant-garde trends of Belgian art at the beginning of the twentieth century. Within it Ensor, Evenpoel and Wouters retained the characteristics of Flemish Expres-

AUGUST MACKE: Wood Engraving

sionism, which had spread to a vast school out of which, after Jean Brusselmans, came the different streams of the new generation. Rik Slabbink came from Brussels; Opsomer was an excellent portrait painter from Antwerp; Och and Scauflaire were typical representatives of Walloon painting; Paul Delvaux (1897—   ) is an existentialist, René Guiette a Cubist, and Victor Servranck a Non-objective painter. The leaders of Belgian painting today are Paul Delvaux and René Magritte. They live and work together with their younger colleagues, Lismonde, Anne Bonnet, etc., in their own country. Alechinsky and Ubac, though living in Paris, are still of the group in which each one can keep his independence.

The young and not-so-young painters of the post-War period are busily at work everywhere, devoting themselves to the 'undefined', and tend to be rather aggressive. Unfortunately, all we can give here is a list of names.

In France, particularly in the School of Paris, there are French painters such as Braque, Manessier, Estève, Gischia, Fautrier, d'Orgaix, Claude George; Russians—de Staël, Poliakoff and Lanskoy; Portuguese—Vieira da Silva; Danes—Richard Mortensen; Belgians (see above)—Bertrand and Singier; Hungarians—Victor Vasarely; Turks—Marius Prassinos; Czechs—Jaroslav Serpan; Canadians—Jean Paul Riopelle; Italian-Swiss—Alberto Giacometti; Chinese—Zao-Wou-Ki—they all live and work in Paris.

In Italy Morandi, Soldati, Prampolini, Spazzapan, Mauro Reggiani, Renato Birolli and other older painters are all artists of repute. Among the younger generation are Achille Perilli, Piero Dorazio, Giovanni Dova and Alberto Brunori. In Spain painters like Tapies, Sauro, Tharrats, Canogar, Feito and Vicente Vela belong to quite a young generation. The Croat Edo Murtic and the Viennese-born Lazaro Vujalklija represent Yugoslavia's contribution to contemporary painting.

RAOUL DUFY: Landscape in the South of France (lithograph)

SALVADOR DALI: Portrait of Mrs Harold F. McCormick (1939, Private Collection, U.S.A.)

Max Ernst: Euclid (1945)

Marc Chagall: Red Sun (1949) →

WILLY BAUMEISTER: Eidos V (1939, Bavarian State Galleries, Munich)

RAOUL DUFY: The Harbour (water-colour)

To the modern German painters (Baumeister, Gilles, Nesch, Scholz, Werner, Nay, Trökes, Schultze and Max Ernst are all of an older generation) we must add the Austrians Hundertwasser, Mikl, Unger and K. A. Wolff (all Viennese), the Swiss—Varlin from Zurich and Bodmer from Basle (Glarner lives in New York) and the Dutch painter Karel Appel. Great Britain's contributions are the works of Ben Nicholson, Hitchens, Sutherland, Francis Bacon, etc., as well as work of younger painters such as Jack Smith, Hamilton Fraser, Harold Cohen, Sandra Blow and Frank Auerbach.

Dutch, Danish, Belgian and Swiss artists are scattered over many countries. In Holland Gerrit Benner and Cornélis van Beverloo (Corneille), thirty years his junior, work closely together. Sweden is represented by a woman of considerable standing, Eva Bergmann; the United States, by such men as de Kooning, Kline, Rothko and Stamos.

Some of the above-mentioned artists, as well as others of the same stature, exhibited at the Biennale of 1960 in Venice. Here we should mention first Hartung (born in Leipzig). He had a comprehensive one-man show of his work of the years between 1942 and 1956, and is the artist who has exercised the greatest influence on non-objective painting of the post-War period. 'Hartung is the painter of Purification, of the new beginning after the Deluge,' said Lorenza Trucchi. Even in the works which show most suffering one feels redemption from anguish, a retreat into serene, one may say religious, silence—a perfect balance.

Another one-man show at the 1960 Biennale was that of Willy Baumeister (1889—1955), who died five years earlier. He was a painter of clearly outlined figurative compositions, within the sphere of the informal. The painter Hans Hofmann (1880—   ), an American citizen since 1947, can still be regarded as a German painter. He was born at Weissenburg in Bavaria. He painted *Fantasy* and *Effervescence*, which both date back to

193

RAOUL DUFY: Reception (detail)
(1942, Louis Carré Collection, Paris)

1943-44, and is, according to the young critics, only a 'minor master.' But it must be noted, that these two canvases are painted in the 'dripping' manner and thus possibly anticipated Pollock by a few years.

Julius Bissier was yet another painter to have a one-man show at the 1960 Biennale. He has a true poetic talent in which the most exquisite elements of old oriental art seem to blend miraculously with those of modern painting.

In the Spanish Pavilion at the 1960 Biennale there may have been too many exhibits. Outstanding among them was the work of Luis Feito, characteristic for its dazzling whites and deep blacks, which lent to these 'biological surfaces,' as one of the critics put it, a most rewarding authenticity.

At the same Biennale we saw works by: Richard Mortensen, the Danish painter, a prolific artist whose development has gone on uninterrupted from 1933; Jan Spychalscki, whose work takes us in retrospect back to the painful years of the War; and the Hungarian Gyula Derkovits, as daring in his choice of subjects as in their execution.

So old and young painters exhibit in Venice, all in search of the hidden nature of things in which they are trying to decipher the hieroglyphics of the structure of matter (Brion). From this it would ensue that we may look upon the artists of today as on a cosmopolitan brotherhood who speak a universal language, an artist's Esperanto.

Charles Bernard, even if not wholly subscribing to this view, still admits to it in part. 'The internationalisation of art presses towards eliminating national elements in favour of unbiased viewing. This and not race

RAOUL DUFY: Love (wood engraving)

from now on determines the nature of a work of art. As long as a work of art had been figurative the question was whether the artist who had executed it was French, English or Spanish, as if the image which the author proposed, independent of the subject, should stand for the image of his country. But today, now that art is non-figurative... '

This, however, is not the main problem. Sedlmayr, in *Die Revolution der Modernen Kunst*, asks whether it is an advantage or not for art to have conformed to the supremacy of inorganic spirit and aestheticism—whether true (*sic*) modern art lives thanks to this or rather in spite of it, and whether such supremacy is acceptable from a human point of view.

'Certainly not,' was the decision of the Congress for Aesthetics which took place at the Theatre of Epidaurus in 1960, in which delegates of many countries participated. The fundamental note of the Congress was the

ANDRÉ DERAIN: Head of a Woman (red chalk)

Lovis Corinth: Self-portrait (drawing)

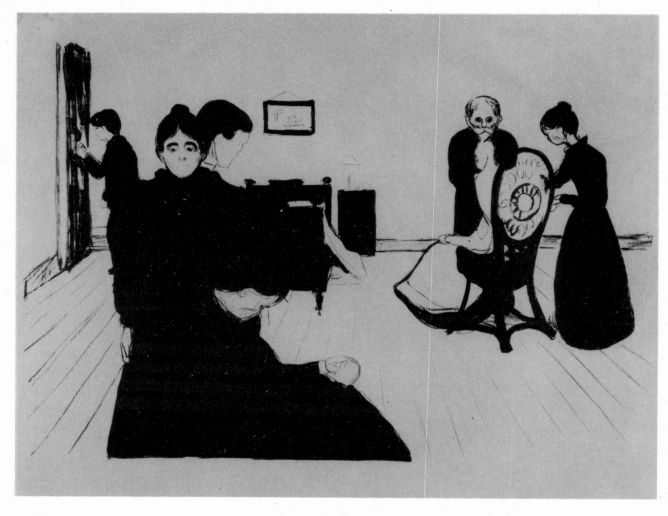

EDVARD MUNCH: The Death-chamber (lithograph)

usual one of modernists versus classicists and the followers of classicism. In these debates, the followers of 'Marxist Aestheticism' were also involved.

The trends of Communist modern art tend towards realism rather than towards abstract art. Realism must be looked upon as a resurrection of the old classical concept of art as an 'imitation and perfection of natural reality'. Therefore Communist art, if it is to remain faithful to Party principles, would have to abnegate Surrealism and the abstract.

Russia's contributions to the 1960 Biennale were (apart from a small group of works by Deinecas, one of the Soviet Realists with a more individual note, and some sculptures by Vera Mukjina) some pleasing genre scenes and landscapes of an Impressionist character.

No need here for explanations! As the whole world is in a state of revolution, so is the world of art! Both the world of reality and the world of art are in a difficult situation. Perhaps charity has gone out of the life of peoples and individuals alike. Fellow-feeling has weakened, if not vanished altogether. This fellow-feeling must be found again in art as well as in life. We have said before that the world of our time, in which symptoms of recent disorder seem still to prevail over hopes for a new order, will be transformed. Art will help to redeem this world, and, in reinstating moral ideals and the forces of the spirit, will direct humanity towards a new harmony.

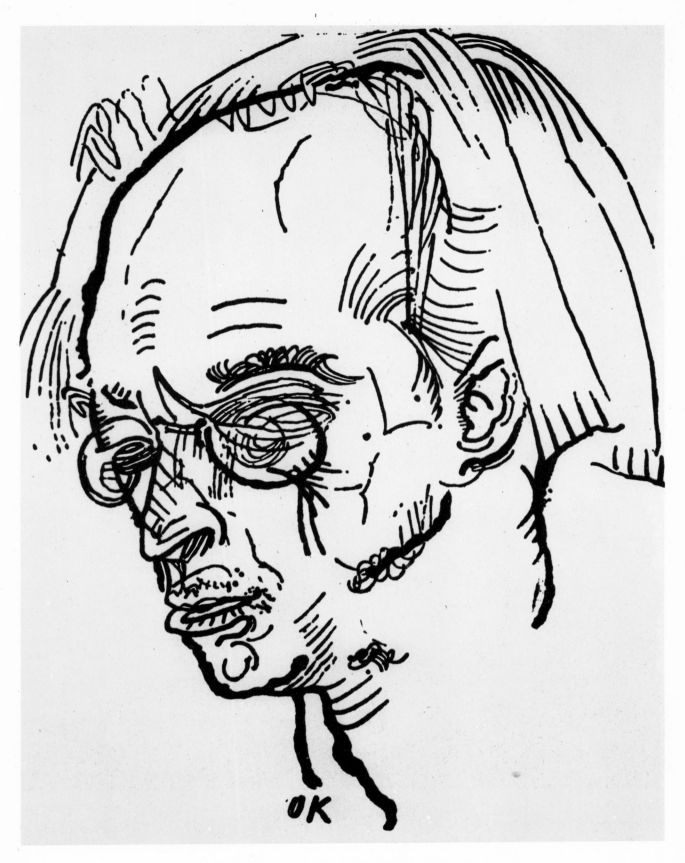

Oskar Kokoschka: Herwarth Walden (drawing)

ERICH HECKEL: Self-portrait (wood engraving)

BIBLIOGRAPHY

LIST OF ILLUSTRATIONS

FRANZ MARC: The Large Blue Horses (1911, Walker Art Center, Minneapolis, Minnesota)

BIBLIOGRAPHY

ALAZARD J.: *L'Orient et la Peinture Française au Dix-neuvième Siècle. D'Eugène Delacroix à Auguste Renoir*, Paris 1930

APOLLONIO, U.: *Panorama dell'Arte Italiana*, Venice 1950

APOLLONIO, U.: in *L'Arte dopo il 1945*, Milan 1959

ARGAN, G. C.—PONENTE, N.: in *L'Arte dopo il 1945*, Milan 1959

BAZIN, G.: *L'Epoque Impressionniste*, Paris 1947

BERNARD, C.: in *L'Arte dopo il 1945*, Milan 1959

BESSON, G.: *L'Impressionnisme et quelques Précurseurs*, Paris 1932

BIE, R.: *Deutsche Malerei der Gegenwart*, 1930

BIHALJI-MERIN, O.: in *L'Arte dopo il 1945*, Milan 1959

BOURET, J.: *Art Abstrait*, Paris 1956

BRION, M.: in *L'Arte dopo il 1945*, Milan 1959

BRIZIO, A. M.: in *Grande Dizionario Enciclopedico*, Turin

BUNT, C.: *Russian Art from Scyths to Soviets*, London 1946

CASSOU, J.: *Die Impressionisten und ihre Zeit*, Munich

CINOTTI, M.: *Arte di tutti i Tempi* (I & II), Novara 1956-7

COGNIAT, R.: *Au Temps des Impressionnistes*, Paris

COLOMBO, A.: *Ecco Leonardo*, Novara 1952

COLOMBO, A.: in *Treasury of World Painting*, New York 1959

DEGAND, L.: *Témoignages pour l'Art Abstrait*, Paris 1952

DIEHL, G.: in *Treasury of World Painting*, New York 1959

DOMNICK, O.: *Die schöpferischen Krafte in der abstrakten Malerei*, Stuttgart-Bergen 1947

DORIVAL, B.: *Les Etapes de la Peinture Française Contemporaine. Tome I: de l'Impressionnisme au Fauvisme*, Paris 1943

DURET, T.: *Histoire des Peintres Impressionnistes*, Paris 1906

DURET, T.: *Les Peintres Impressionnistes*, Paris 1878

FAURE, E.: *L'Histoire de l'Art*, Paris 1921

FORMAGGIO, D.: *Otto Secoli di Pittura*, Novara 1956

FRANCASTEL, P.: *La Peinture de Chevalet du XIVe au XXe Siècle*, Paris 1955

FRANCASTEL, P.: *L'Impressionnisme—Les Origines de la Peinture Moderne de Monet à Gauguin*, Paris 1937

GEFFROY, G.: 'Histoire de l'Impressionnisme.' *La Vie Artistique*, Paris 1894

GIBELLINO KRASCENINNICOWA, M.: *Storia dell'Arte Russa*, Rome 1935

GRISEBACH, A.: *Grundzüge der französischen Kunst*, 1947

GROHMANN, W.: in *L'Arte dopo il 1945*, Milan 1959

HAMANN, R.: *Der Impressionismus in Leben und Kunst*, Marburg 1923

HARTLAUB, G. F.: *Die Graphik des Expressionismus in Deutschland*, 1947

HAUSENSTEIN, W.: *Die bildende Kunst der Gegenwart*, 1920

HAUSENSTEIN, W.: *Was bedeutet die moderne Kunst?* 1949

HERMANIN, H.: *Gli Artisti Italiani in Germania*, Rome 1953

HESS, W.: *Dokumente zum Verständnis der Modernen Malerei*, Hamburg 1956

HILDEBRANDT, H.: 'Die Kunst des 19. und 20. Jahrhunderts.' *Handbuch der Kunstgeschichte*, 1925

HODIN, J. P.: in *L'Arte dopo il 1945*, Milan 1959

HUYGHE, R.: 'Genèse et Position de l'Art Moderne.' *L'Amour de l'Art*, Paris 1933

JAFFE, H. L. C.: in *L'Arte dopo il 1945*, Milan 1959

JEDLICKA, G.: *Begegnungen mit Künstlern der Gegenwart*, 1945

JEWELL, E. A.: *French Impressionists and their Contemporaries*, New York 1946

JIMENEZ, Placer-Suarez De Lezo: *Historia del Arte Español*, Madrid 1955

JUSTI, L.: *Von Corinth bis Klee*, 1931

KHWOSHINSKI-SALMI: *I Pittori Toscani*, Rome 1912

LEGENDRE, M.—Harris, E.: *La Peinture Espagnole*, Paris 1937

LINDBLOM, A.: *Sveriges Konsthistoria*, Stockholm 1944

MARCHIORI, G.: *Panorama dell'Arte Italiana*, Turin 1951

MARX, Cl. Roger: *Un Siècle d'Art*, Paris 1900

MAUCLAIR, C.: *L'Impressionnisme, son Histoire, son Esthétique, ses Maîtres*, Paris 1904

MEIER-GRAEFE, J.: *Entwicklungsgeschichte der modernen Kunst*, Stuttgart 1904, Munich 1927

MEIER-GRAEFE, J.: *Entwicklungsgeschichte der modernen Kunst*, 1920

MEYER, P.: *Europäische Kunstgeschichte*, Zürich 1948

MICHEL, A.: *Histoire de l'Art*, Paris 1921-4

NOVOTNY, F.: *Die grossen französischen Impressionisten. Ihre Vorläufer und Nachläufer*, Vienna

RAYNAL: *Histoire de la Peinture Moderne, de Baudelaire à Bonnard*, Geneva 1950

READ, H.: *A Concise History of Modern Painting*, London 1959

READ, H.: in *L'Arte dopo il 1945*, Milan 1959

REINACH, S.: *Apollo*

REWALD, J.: *The History of Impressionism*, New York 1946

REY, R.: *La Peinture Française à la fin du XIXe Siècle. La Renaissance du sentiment Classique*, Paris 1931

REY, R.: 'Les Disciples de l'Impressionnisme.' *L'Amour de l'Art*, Paris 1933

RICKERT, M.: *Painting in Britain*, London 1954

RITCHIE, A. C.: *Masters of British Painting*, London 1956

ROTHEL, H. K.: *Moderne deutsche Malerei*, Wiesbaden 1957

ROTHENSTEIN, J.: *Nineteenth-Century Painting*, London 1932

SAUERLANDT, M.: *Die Kunst der letzten dreissig Jahre (bis 1933)*, 1948

SCHMIDT, K. E.: *Französische Malerei des 19. Jahrhunderts*, Leipzig 1903

SCHMIDT, P. F.: *Die Kunst der Gegenwart*, 1922

SEDLMAYR, H.: *Verlust der Mitte*, Munich 1950

SEDLMAYR, H.: in *Rowohlts Deutsche Enzyklopädie*, Munich 1955

SOMARÈ, E.: *La Pittura Italiana dell'Ottocento*, Novara 1944

STIX, A.: *Von Ingres bis Cézanne. 32 Handzeichnungen französischer Meister des 19. Jahrhunderts aus der Albertina*, Vienna 1927

SYDOW, E. v.: *Die deutsche expressionistische Kultur und Malerei*, 1920

UHDE, W.: *Die Impressionisten*, Vienna 1937

VALSECCHI, M.: *Profilo della Pittura Moderna*, Milan 1959

VENTURI, L.: *Come si comprende la Pittura: da Giotto a Chagall*, Rome 1956

VENTURI, L.: *Les Archives de l'Impressionnisme*, Paris 1939

WALDMANN, E.: *Die Kunst des Realismus und des Impressionismus im 19. Jahrhundert*, Berlin 1927

WEIGERT, H.: *Holländische Malerei*, Stuttgart 1959

WILENSKI, R. H.: *English Painting*, London 1933

WILENSKI, R. H.: *French Painting*, Boston 1931

WILENSKI, R. H.: *Modern French Painters*, London-New York 1940

WILENSKI, R. H.: *Modern French Painters*, New York 1947

WOERMANN, K.: *Geschichte der Kunst*, 1922

Other authors are mentioned in the text.

PAUL KLEE: Intention (1938, Klee-Stiftung, Berne)

LIST OF ILLUSTRATIONS

Printed in Italy — Istituto Geografico De Agostini S.p.A. - Novara - 1961